HIDDEN HISTORY

HISTORY

of

KENSINGTON

&

FISHTOWN

HIDDEN
HISTORY

of

KENSINGTON

&

FISHTOWN

KENNETH W. MILANO

THE
History
PRESS

Published by The History Press
Charleston, SC 29403
www.historypress.net

Back cover: postcard of the Cramp Shipyard. Courtesy of the author.
Unless otherwise specified, the images for this book come
from the privatecollectionof the author.

First published 2010

Manufactured in the United States
ISBN 978.1.60949.103.1

Library of Congress Cataloging-in-Publication Data
Milano, Kenneth W.
Hidden history of Kensington and Fishtown / Kenneth W. Milano.
p. cm.
Includes bibliographical references.
ISBN 978-1-60949-103-1
1. Kensington (Philadelphia, Pa.)--History. 2. Fishtown (Philadelphia, Pa.)--History. 3.
Kensington (Philadelphia, Pa.)--Social conditions. 4. Fishtown (Philadelphia, Pa.)--Social
conditions. 5. Kensington (Philadelphia, Pa.)--Biography. 6. Fishtown (Philadelphia,
Pa.)--Biography. 7. Philadelphia (Pa.)--History. 8. Philadelphia (Pa.)--Social conditions. 9.
Philadelphia (Pa.)--Biography. I. Title.
F158.68.K46M3 2010
974.8'11--dc22
2010039760

This book is dedicated to the working-class families of Kensington and Fishtown who have made the neighborhoods such great places to live, work and raise our families. They should be proud of the rich history they have contributed to. I also dedicate this book to the newer residents who are adding yet another chapter to the history of the area.

Contents

CONTENTS

Foreword

The streets of Fishtown and Kensington are thoroughfares literally laid on the foundations of American history. And with those centuries of accumulated history come volumes of buried stories and mysteries.

Leaving the neat little grid of squares mapped out by William Penn in 1682, it's impossible to miss the tangled maze of streets just northeast of Center City that make up these neighborhoods. Crooked roads, patches of exposed cobblestone, long-abandoned rail lines, vacant or reinvented industrial palaces and streets with names like "Shackamaxon" and "Aramingo" all tell the tale of a place where the history is profound.

For the generations of families that call these neighborhoods home, the sense of past and mystery is a source of personal, family pride and a source of local lore. Those families settled these lands, fished the Delaware's shad, worked in the factories and are buried in the neighborhood's storied Palmer Cemetery. But as the neighborhoods continue to transition from their recent industrial past to a fashionable quarter where expensive condos and stylish restaurants are flourishing, new residents are equally drawn to the ancient and mysterious qualities of this place.

Guiding the curious from each camp is Ken Milano, lifelong resident of Kensington, passionate historian, professional genealogist and prolific writer. Each week, residents of these neighborhoods turn to Milano's "The Rest Is History" column in the *Fishtown Star*, a weekly paper serving the neighborhoods since the 1970s. The essays published in the *Star* were the inspiration behind several History Press books, including *Remembering Fishtown and Kensington: Philadelphia's Riverward Neighborhoods*, *The History of The Kensington Soup Society* and *The History of Penn Treaty Park*.

Each of those books took Milano's original writings and expanded upon them, digging deeper into the past and providing more detail and more background. This latest book, *Hidden History of Kensington and Fishtown*, digs still deeper, offering an in-depth look at the obscure but important stories that add considerably to the rich canon of history in two of Philadelphia's oldest and most significant neighborhoods.

Indeed, one can find elements of American history in Fishtown stretching back to the earliest of eras—starting with the continent's first humans. It was here, after all, that archaeologists uncovered a trove of hundreds of Native American artifacts in 2008, some dating back as far as 3,500 years. On these pages, Milano illustrates that past through the lens of "Point Pleasant," a stretch of the Delaware River banks in Fishtown where area tribes convened and a complex ferry system thrived well before the first Europeans arrived.

It's telling that the site of another important yet little-known piece of American history, "Batchelor's Hall," rests on these same banks. In few other books will you find such detailed information about one of our nation's first philosophical meeting places—a rowdy hall where friends of Benjamin Franklin threw around ideas with John Bartram, an early and important American botanist.

Here, too, readers will find accounts of impressive British military outposts, Fishtown residents turned Revolutionary War heroes and raucous street protests starring America's first citizens. Later, Milano captures the area's past as an industrial powerhouse, looking at everything from the start of Hero Fruit Jar Company to the great Bromley family carpet mills. Readers can also visit the Kensington row home where the mighty Knights of Labor union began in 1869 and read detailed accounts of the violent Cramp Shipyard Strike of the 1920s.

Even more obscure are the tales of the rolling gang fights that plagued the neighborhoods not in the 1980s but in the 1880s. Throw in stories of bank robbers, embezzlement, the bizarre double suicide committed by the violent Rusk twins and the "Speakeasy War" of 1890, and you glimpse a dark side of our history not found elsewhere.

Milano also takes care to chronicle underappreciated heroes, such as Eddie Stanky, a second baseman with the iconic 1951 New York Giants best known for his finicky at-bats and ability to draw hundreds of walks at the plate. Before he was a national figure, he was simply known as the "Brat from Kensington."

Buried and largely unknown nuggets of the past such as these make *Hidden History of Kensington and Fishtown* an impressive addition to what seemed an already exhaustive chronicling of local history on the part of Milano.

Still, there is a sense of irony in this collection of stories: nearly all of the history of Fishtown and Kensington has long been "hidden" in the shadow of nearby historic giants like Independence Hall and the Liberty Bell. But for those whose curiosity brings them beyond the evident, Milano's research and writing provide an invaluable guide to this intriguing and storied section of Philadelphia.

Brian Rademaekers lives in Kensington and is the editor of the Fishtown Star.

Acknowledgements

None of the work I do is without the help and knowledge of my colleagues in the Kensington History Project, Torben Jenk and Rich Remer. I would like to thank these two gentlemen for the many years of collaborative research and fellowship in all things Kensington and Fishtown.

I would also like to thank Doug Mooney, senior archaeologist for URS Corporation, Inc. Doug supplied me with photographs taken by URS of artifacts and archaeological digs that were carried out in the neighborhood. These images are used by permission of the Pennsylvania Department of Transportation District 6-0 and were funded by the Federal Highway Administration (FHWA).

Frank O'Connor deserves a thank-you for introducing me to the history of the A.C. Harmer Club. Frank was once a member of a club that owned the old A.C. Harmer Club's building and long ago found in the building's attic ledgers of the Harmer Club's minute meetings, allowing me to unearth the previously unknown history of the organization.

Thanks also to Daniel Dailey for the use of the Cramp Shipyard workers photograph. While researching the image, we discovered it to have been taken at the intersection of Norris and Claiborne Streets. Claiborne Street is long vacant. Dailey's collection of historical artifacts and memorabilia of Kensington and Fishtown is becoming unmatched by any other.

Tom Prince, a local Civil War reenactor, deserves a thank-you for introducing me to St. Anne's Civil War hero Lieutenant Colonel Peter McAloon.

Also, big thanks go out to my editor at the *Fishtown Star*, Brian Rademaekers, whose commitment to the "Rest Is History" column is a large part of my continued success. I also need to thank all the readers of my column for their continued support. There is hardly a day that goes by when I am not stopped on the street, at the supermarket or even approached while sitting on my stoop by people thanking me for telling the neighborhood's history.

Last, but certainly not least, I thank my wife, Dorina, my two boys, Francesco and Salvatore, and my mother, Marie, without whom life on York Street would not be nearly as "interesting" or "fun."

CHAPTER I

Kensington in Olden Times

ORIGINS OF THE WORD SHACKAMAXON

Shackamaxon is the name for the ancient Native American settlement that is now occupied by the Philadelphia neighborhoods of Fishtown, Kensington and Port Richmond. Since the seventeenth century, historians and linguists have argued over the origins of the word Shackamaxon. The earliest mention of Shackamaxon appears to be by Peter Lindstrom, a seventeenth-century Swedish engineer who sailed down the Delaware River compiling a survey of the Delaware Valley in 1654–55. At this time, Lindstrom titled the Leni-Lenape settlement at Shackamaxon on his map as "Kacamensi."

Lindstrom's map was printed in a 1925 translation of his work called *Geographia Americae, with an account of the Delaware Indians based on Surveys and Notes made in 1654-1655.* The work is an interesting piece, particularly for the "contact period" when Native Americans and Europeans were living side by side.

Some linguists think Shackamaxon to be derived from "shachamek," "shakamik" or "w'shackamek," which literally means "it is a straight fish"—an eel. The suffix "ink," or in this case "mek" or "mik," is said to mean "at or where." Hence, Shackamaxon would mean "at the place of eels." Since eels were plentiful in the Delaware River, the meaning had some substance. However, there is a larger group of linguists that has seemed to win the argument. They have placed Shackamaxon as being derived from "sakima," "sachemen," meaning "chief, or king" and with the suffix "ink" meaning "at" or "where"; hence, Shackamaxon would be translated as "where the kings are" or "at the meeting place of kings" or, in the Native American context, "chiefs."

This later definition would appear to hold more weight, particularly when looking at the history of Shackamaxon, as it was known to be the place where regular tribal councils were held. Shackamaxon was also the place where, in 1682, Tammanend, as the head sachem of the Turtle clan of the Unami tribe of the Leni-Lenape, made his "treaty of amity and friendship" with William Penn, the founder of Pennsylvania. It was an event that is memorialized by today's Penn Treaty Park.

Tammanend belonged to the Native American peoples called the Leni-Lenape. There were three groups within the Lenape. The northernmost group of the Lenapes, the Munsee group, occupied the area where the Delaware River begins, or where Pennsylvania, New Jersey and New York come together. The Unami, the central group of Tammanend, occupied the northern region and central New Jersey and the adjoining portions of eastern Pennsylvania woodland along the Delaware River and parts inland. The Unami southern border reached to an area just below today's city of Philadelphia. The southernmost group, the Unalactigo, inhabited both sides of the lower Delaware River below Philadelphia, including the Delaware Bay area and what would currently be northern Delaware, southeast Pennsylvania and South Jersey.

Besides the Lenape being made up of three territorial groups, there were also three different matrilineal clans that were present in the groups: the Turtle, Wolf and Turkey. The Turtle Clan was the most important, and usually the sachem, or chief of the tribal councils, was from this clan. Thus, Tammanend was the tribal council leader, and it was he who treated with William Penn at the Lenape's capital of Shackamaxon.

Hopefully, the recent archaeological investigations at the SugarHouse site, as well as the archaeological investigations by URS Corporation for the Pennsylvania Department of Transportation's expansion of Interstate 95, will help us to find out more about the original inhabitants of these neighborhoods of Shackamaxon.

Today, the name of Shackamaxon has all but disappeared. Fishtown still has a street honoring the ancient Lenape settlement of Shackamaxon, and while Shackamaxon Street today runs from Frankford Avenue to the

Overview of excavations of Remer Site, 1028–1030 Shackmaxon Street. *Courtesy of the Pennsylvania Department of Transportation, District 6-0 and the Federal Highways Administration.*

Delaware River, butting up against the SugarHouse Casino site, it wasn't always that way.

Shackamaxon Street was originally cut out only from Frankford Avenue to Richmond Street, the rest of the way being private land. Shackamaxon Street probably represents one of the oldest streets in Fishtown. There is some evidence that it actually may have been called "Greenwood Lane," after an early property owner, before changing to Shackamaxon.

Shackamaxon Street dates to at least the 1750s, as Rich Remer, one of the founders of the Kensington History Project and a colleague of this author, dates his original ancestry back to the 1000 block of Shackamaxon. This Shackamaxon Street home was the original home of his ancestor, Godfrey Remer, who emigrated from the Rhineland as a teenager. Godfrey occupied the house by the 1760s and 1770s, and Remer reports that it was built in the 1750s. It sits next to Interstate 95 and was lucky to survive the bulldozing of the neighborhood when the highway was built.

POINT PLEASANT, TERMINUS OF ANCIENT NATIVE AMERICAN TRANSPORTATION ROUTES

It wasn't just a fluke that during the American Revolution the British happened to occupy Point Pleasant during their occupation of Philadelphia in the winter of 1777–78. Today's site of the SugarHouse Casino always held strategic importance, going back to ancient times, due to the confluence of major roads and river travel routes.

It turns out that this area of Kensington, known then as "Point Pleasant," was always strategic for Native Americans. Several ancient routes of the

Portion of map showing ancient Native American trails in Pennsylvania, with many leading to the Leni-Lenape capital of Shackamaxon.

Leni-Lenape all converged on this site. The ancient Indian trails of what would become known to the Europeans as Germantown and Frankford Roads both ended at Point Pleasant. Old York Road, another ancient Native American trail, connected with Germantown Road just prior to joining up with Frankford Avenue. There was also an old Native American ferry system of canoes that connected Shackamaxon to other Lenape settlements on the New Jersey side of the Delaware River.

The archaeological investigations that have been conducted on the SugarHouse site have found an intact Native American site, dating back to about 1500 BC. There are only several Native American sites that have ever been identified in the inner city (the heavily built up area) of Philadelphia, and with this site being so close to the site of William Penn's famed Treaty with the Indians (Penn Treaty Park), it offers a unique opportunity not only to understand the history of the Native Americans before the Europeans arrived, the "precontact

Arrowhead excavated from northwest corner of Columbia and Delaware Avenues. *Courtesy of the Pennsylvania Department of Transportation, District 6-0 and the Federal Highways Administration.*

period," but also to understand the fifty-plus years of the "contact period," when the Europeans lived side by side with the Native Americans.

Before William Cooper ever started his ferry from Camden, New Jersey, to Shackamaxon, the Lenape already had in place their own canoe ferry from their Arasapha settlement on the Jersey shore to Shackamaxon on the western shore of the river. This fact is recorded in several books, including George R. Prowell's mammoth *History of Camden County*, which states, "Intercourse between Shackamaxon, where the pioneers of Penn's colony, under Fairman, the surveyor, and Markham, the deputy-governor, and Pyne Point [Camden County] had long been established by canoe ferry between the Indian settlements at those places."

Prowell goes on to say that William Cooper (who took over this Lenape ferry after the arrival of the Europeans) was "present at the treaty of Penn with the Indians in 1682, at Shackamaxon, opposite his house." Cooper's ferry house at Pyne Point (Camden) still survives, and one can see it in the distance from the Delaware River shore at the SugarHouse site.

The ferry between the New Jersey side of the river, where the Native Americans originally had a settlement at Camden called Arasapha, and a point on the SugarHouse site at Shackamaxon Street landing lasted throughout much of the history of this site. Much later, the Kensington and New Jersey Ferry Company was organized in 1866 by local shipbuilders William Cramp, Jacob Neafie and others. They operated a ferry between Camden and Shackamaxon Street. The company began operating its first boat, the *Shackamaxon*, on July 28, 1866.

Point Pleasant, today's SugarHouse Casino, was a major terminus for ancient routes of the Native Americans. Is it any wonder, then, that only four inches underground archaeologists have found American Indian artifacts over thirty-five hundred years old?

WINDOW TO THE REVOLUTION: JOHN HEWSON, ELIZABETH FARMER, ROBERT MORTON AND LIEUTENANT COLONEL JOHN GRAVES SIMCOE

One of Kensington's most famous Revolutionary spirits was John Hewson. Hewson was born in 1744 in England, the son of a London woolen draper. He descended from Colonel John Hewson, a supporter of Oliver Cromwell who

Contemporary portrait painting of John Hewson (1744–1821), calico printer, Revolutionary War hero and founder of Kensington Methodist Episcopal "Old Brick" Church. *Courtesy of Todd Fielding.*

was implicated in the execution of King Charles I. Like his famous ancestor, and to the dismay of his parents, young John Hewson held extreme political views. Republican tendencies did not fare well under King George III, and Hewson's parents—with the help of that most famous of Philadelphians, Benjamin Franklin—were able to get young John to immigrate to America in 1774.

Hewson was trained as a printer of calico fabrics and had worked for Talwin & Foster, a leading English textile printworks, at Bromley Hall near London. He very likely brought his equipment to Philadelphia, and perhaps half a dozen workmen as well. He opened a calico-printing factory in 1774, near the Delaware River at the foot of Gunner's Run, now Aramingo Avenue, in Kensington. At that time, Richmond Street was called Point-no-Point Road, and Hewson's address was listed on the Point Road, near today's Hewson Street, which was named for him.

Not only was Hewson one of the earliest calico fabric printers in the colonies, but his work was also of the highest quality. According to scholars of textile history, Hewson's textiles were unmatched in America at that time and rivaled those of Europe. His textiles were expensive and highly sought after for dresses, furnishing fabrics and handkerchiefs. Even today, Hewson is still considered one of the finest craftsmen in American textile printing history.

In 1775, Martha Washington paid a visit to John Hewson at Kensington. Mrs. Washington's relative, William Ball, who owned the property on which Hewson's factory stood, lived near Hewson. Mrs. Washington had heard of Hewson's fabrics and paid him a visit to commission on a handkerchief an image of her husband on horseback. It is said that Mrs. Washington eventually became a regular patron of and visitor to Hewson's calico printing factory.

At the outbreak of the American Revolution, John Hewson, already a vocal supporter of the Patriot cause, enrolled in the First Republican Grenadiers in 1775. After this group disbanded, he was commissioned an officer, formed a company of men out of his Kensington factory workers and had himself attached to the county militia.

Hewson had to flee Philadelphia for New Jersey when the British landed and occupied the city in late September 1777. British soldiers sacked Hewson's Kensington office and factory, and he narrowly escaped with some of his tools, machinery and animals by taking a boat off the Kensington shore, leaving Kensington just before the British arrived. He was eventually captured in New Jersey and, after spending some time in Philadelphia's Walnut Street Prison, was transferred to New York. After a brief imprisonment there, he managed to escape, almost drowning in the process.

An excerpt from his diary, in the collections at the Historical Society of Pennsylvania, tells the story of his escape:

> *When the British Army approached near to the city I removed with my family to the Jerseys about 4 miles from Cooper's Ferry; with my household furniture and as many of my manufacturing utensils as the shortness of the time would permit me to take, such as Copper boilers, and a large leaden vessel used in souring the goods we printed weighing several hundred pounds with as many of my valuable prints, mahogany printing tables, blankets, tearing tubs, broadcloth, sieves, brushes, etc, as I could hurry off with also 3 cows and 2 horses and poultry, such as fowls & ducks plenty, which we*

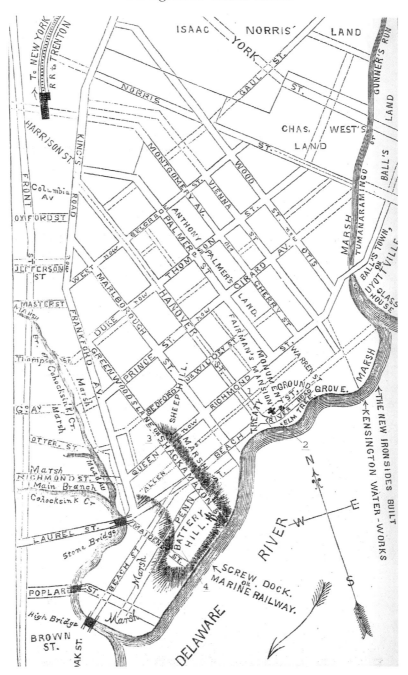

Map showing distance from Treaty Elm Tree to Simcoe's British Redoubt No. 1, seen here as Battery Hill. *Courtesy of Sloan's Architectural Journal & Builder's Review, 1868.*

shut up in boxes, chests, and by time we got over the river they half died for want of air to breathe in while we were loading a large boat at the wharf, we was obliged to have a person on the top of the chimney to look out the van of the army being at Frankford, I was under the necessity of leaving a great many things behind me.

When the war was over, Hewson set about restoring his business. Because of his patriotism and his daring escapes, he was seen as a local war hero. During the Grand Federal Procession on July 4, 1788, Hewson was honored in the parade, traveling at the center of the manufacturers' float.

In 1790, the Manufacturing Society awarded Hewson a gold medal for the best example of calico printing in the state. He retired from his business in 1810 and helped to found Kensington Methodist Episcopal "Old Brick" Church. John Hewson died in 1821 and is buried on the north side of the Palmer Cemetery, near the Montgomery Street gate, a true Kensington Patriot.

As Captain Hewson's biography shows, Kensington had a role in the American Revolution. Besides Hewson's short diary that exists recounting some of his Revolutionary War experiences, there is also other evidence—letters, other contemporary diaries and maps—that illustrates Kensington's role during the war.

Elizabeth Farmer was one such Kensingtonian who left a record of the war in the neighborhood. She lived in the Bower Mansion, previously located at the southwest corner of Frankford Avenue and Norris Street, roughly behind today's clubhouse for the Warlock's Motorcycle Club. During that cold winter of 1777, the winter of Valley Forge fame, she wrote letters to her cousin describing the "picquets" of the British and American soldiers who were skirmishing outside her house, some stealing her fence for firewood. Firewood was scarce in the area, it was an exceptionally cold winter that year and many of the trees had been felled in the outlying districts of Philadelphia (including Kensington) by the British for use to fortify their defense of the city, as well as to clear the sight lines for their soldiers.

An entry in Robert Morton's diary for November 22, 1777, confirms Elizabeth Farmer's accounts. Morton's diary states that the British "set fire to Fair Hill Mansion…and many others…The reason they assign for this destruction of property is on account of the Americans firing from these houses and harassing their Picquets."

The Fairhill Mansion was the mansion house of the old Isaac Norris estate, then held by John Dickinson and located at today's Marshall and York Streets. Americans were using the mansion for cover while sniping at the British scouts. Besides Fairhill, many other buildings in the countryside of Kensington were burned and destroyed by the British, as were businesses along the riverfront, like Peter Browne's smith shop and the Eyre brothers' shipyard.

Morton's diary also mentions the British defense works that they built across the northern border of the city, running roughly along the line where Poplar Street is today, from the Schuylkill to the Delaware Rivers. There

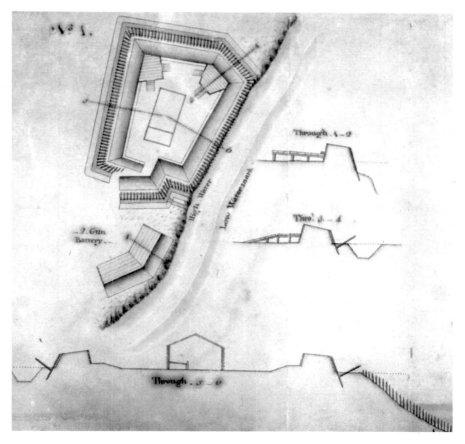

Part of Lewis Nicola's map of 1777, with overhead and side views of Kensington's British Redoubt No. 1 with defenses of felled trees and moat.

Portrait of Lieutenant Colonel John Graves Simcoe (1752–1806), commander of the Queen's Rangers and stationed at Kensington's British Redoubt No. 1 from September 1777 to June 1778.

were "ten redoubts, connected by strong palisades." The easternmost point of this line was British Redoubt No. 1, located on the riverbank of the Delaware, between Frankford Avenue and Shackamaxon Street, on a line with today's Laurel Street.

British lieutenant colonel John Graves Simcoe, who commanded the British troops at Kensington's British Redoubt No. 1, posted some men from his Queen's Rangers, a Loyalist group, near the famous Penn's Treaty Tree. Simcoe, aware of the Treaty Tree's significance, did not want anyone chopping it down for firewood. Simcoe also recruited in Philadelphia for the Queen's Rangers, as evidenced by an advertisement placed in a local Philadelphia newspaper in March 1778.

A journal, kept by Simcoe and dated October 1777, recounts his stay in Kensington during the war:

QUEEN's RANGERS.

ALL young and able-bodied MEN, (seafaring men excepted) who are desirous of serving their KING and COUNTRY, during the present rebellion, will repair to the commanding officer's quarters of the Queen's Rangers at Kensington, where they will receive their full bounty, cloathing, arms and accoutrements.

Advertisement for recruits for Lieutenant Colonel Simcoe's Queen's Rangers, quartered at British Redoubt No. 1 at Kensington. Pennsylvania Ledger, *March 18, 1778.*

The village of Kensington was several times attacked by the rebel patrolling parties; they could come by means of the woods very near to it undiscovered; there was a road over a small creek to Point-no-Point; to defend this a house was made musket proof, and the bridge taken up; cavalry only approached to this post, for it lying, as has been mentioned, in an angle between the Delaware and the Frankfort road, infantry were liable to be cut off; on the left there was a knoll that overlooked the country; this was the post of the piquet in the daytime, but corn fields high enough to conceal the approach of an enemy reached to its basis; sentinels from hence inclined to the left and joined those of Colonel Twistleton's light infantry of the guards, so that this hill projected forward, and on that account was ordered by Sir William Erskine not to be defended if attacked in force, and it was withdrawn at night...At night the corps was drawn back to the houses nearer Philadelphia, and guards were placed behind breastworks, made by heaping up the fences in such points as commanded the avenues to the village; (which was laid out and enclosed in right angles) these were themselves overlooked by others that constituted the alarm post of the different companies. Fires also were made in particular places before the piquet, to discover whatsoever should approach. Before day the whole corps was under arms, and remained so till the piquets returned to their day post, which they resumed, taking every precaution against ambuscades; the light infantry of the guards advanced their piquets at the same time, and Colonel Twistleton was an admirable pattern for attention and spirit, to all who served with him.

Simcoe's description of his northern defensive positions in Kensington is well illustrated in a contemporary map drawn by Lewis Nicola in November 1777. Nicola's map clearly shows the British defense lines across the northern part of Philadelphia, as well as their defensive positions on the northern side of the Cohocksink Creek, Kensington's historic southern border. In particular, the "British Fort No. 1" is found on Nicola's map and is located at the exact site of where the SugarHouse Casino is located today.

CAPTAIN PETER BROWNE, REVOLUTIONARY WAR BLACKSMITH

While researching the Point Pleasant area of Kensington and the history of Batchelor's Hall, I came across the orderly book of Revolutionary War soldier Peter Browne (1751–1810), a local Kensingtonian and an American Patriot whose story is not widely known.

Browne was the son of Nathaniel Browne (1726–1800) and his first wife, Mary Burdsall (d. 1754), and the grandson of Peter Browne (d. 1749) and Sarah Fisher (d. circa 1735). After the early death of his grandmother, Browne's grandfather remarried the widow of James Parrock Jr., Priscilla Parrock (d. 1745), whose father was William Coats, a large landowner in the Northern Liberties area of then Philadelphia County. Coats owned much of the current-day neighborhood of Northern Liberties. He had come into half of Jurian Hartsfelder's 350-acre tract, which sat just north of Vine Street on the Delaware River, a tract that Hartsfelder had owned even before the arrival of William Penn.

Nathaniel Browne had been bred a blacksmith, and upon the coming of age of his son Peter, he bought a property in Kensington. It was here that he built a blacksmith shop for his son. It appears to have been a shop that serviced the maritime trade, a shipsmithry.

The shop was located on Queen Street (now Richmond) between Palmer and Montgomery Streets and ran from Queen to the low-water mark of the Delaware River. In May 1777, Nathaniel Browne transferred this shop to his son Peter, who took over the Kensington business.

When the movement for American independence started, Peter Browne became involved early on. In the summer of 1775, he became one of the associates with the rank of first lieutenant in the First Battalion of City

Associators, under Colonel John Dickinson. Dickinson had married into Isaac Norris's family and occupied Fairhill Mansion, which was located at about today's Marshall and York Streets. Fairhill Mansion was burned and sacked by the British during the war.

Peter Browne appears to have seen service with the associators at Amboy in 1775 and in 1777; he became a member of fellow Kensingtonian Captain Jehu Eyre's company of artillery. Eyre owned a shipyard with his two brothers (Manuel and Benjamin) very near to Peter Browne's blacksmith shop in Kensington. Today's Eyre Street is named for this family. Peter was also at this time "furnishing iron work" on the Pennsylvania fire vessels that were being built to patrol the Delaware River and is also recorded as supervising six other blacksmiths who were working on a bridge that was being built over the Schuylkill River.

After six months' service under Captain Eyre, Browne was promoted to a captain when Eyre was made commander of the artillery battalion. Peter served during the war at Fort Billingsport in September 1777 and at Whitemarsh two months later. It was at this time at Whitemarsh that there survives Browne's orderly book. Whitemarsh was the last major engagement of 1777, before Washington settled into winter quarters at Valley Forge.

The British army sacked Browne's blacksmith shop during the winter of 1777–78. It was during this time that the British occupied Philadelphia, running their main northern defense line through the southern part of Kensington and building what came to be known as British Redoubt No. 1 at today's SugarHouse Casino site. After the war, Browne put in a claim for £3,110, the fourth-highest claim in the Northern Liberties (which Kensington was included in at that time).

One of those with a higher claim than Browne was Jehu Eyre, Browne's commander. Eyre had his shipyard sacked and two ships taken, not to mention the lumber that was lost. Eyre's damages were said to be £6,392. He was never reimbursed, and from his time in the war his health became poor. He died shortly after, in 1781.

After the war, Peter Browne continued the blacksmith shop in Kensington, but he also had another shop at 141 North Front Street and a wharf and lumberyard on the river between Arch and Race Streets. He brought his son John Coats Browne (1774–1832) into business with him. John C. Browne eventually became the first president of the Kensington National Bank, which was originally located on Point Pleasant's Beach Street before moving to Frankford

PETER BROWNE'S COAT OF ARMS.

Peter Browne's coat of arms with the inscription "By This I Got Ye," a reference to the anvil image. He was a blacksmith. *Courtesy of Torben Jenk.*

and Girard Avenues. John C. Browne also became a one-time president of the Board of Commissioners of Kensington at a time when Kensington was self-governing, thus effectively making him the "mayor" of Kensington.

Peter Browne died in 1810 and was buried at the Old Coates Burial Ground at Third and Brown Streets but was later removed to Laurel Hill Cemetery.

KENSINGTON'S PROTEST OF JAY'S TREATY, 1795

One of the more interesting social disturbances that took place in Kensington was an incident that occurred after the announcement of Jay's Treaty in 1795.

John Jay (1745–1829) was a New Yorker and one of America's founding fathers. He served the American cause in many capacities: president of the Continental Congress, the first chief justice of the United States and secretary of foreign affairs, among other distinguished honors. Despite all his accolades, Jay is best remembered by many for Jay's Treaty (1795). This treaty, between the United States and England, helped to avert another war at the time it was made. The treaty was supposed to address many issues left over from the Revolutionary War; however, it did not, and the averted war eventually took place, known today as the War of 1812.

Jay's Treaty was disliked by many. It was one of the main reasons for the first party system developing in America. Federalists, supported by Alexander Hamilton and John Jay, advocated for a strong national government, while Democratic-Republicans, supported by Thomas Jefferson and James Madison, advocated for constrained government powers with strong states' rights.

Hamilton drafted Jay's Treaty, and with the support of President Washington, Jay was sent to London to negotiate it. The treaty addressed many things: British occupation of western forts (in Ohio), compensation for American ships seized by the British, England getting "most favored nation" status and America paying pre–Revolutionary War debts, among other issues. One issue not resolved was the business of English impressments of American sailors into the Royal Navy, an issue that would later become a key problem leading to the War of 1812.

Kensington in 1795 was a maritime suburb of Philadelphia, with many men making their living by the sea. It was an area always known for its dislike for strong national government, and hence, many were supporters of Jefferson and Madison. Jay leaving out the impressments issue in the treaty infuriated the men from Kensington. When the announcement was made of what Jay's Treaty did and did not include, Kensingtonians took to the streets.

According to the *Independent Gazetteer* of July 8, 1795, Kensingtonians held a Fourth of July parade that resembled a funeral:

> *The birth day of American liberty was celebrated in this City with a funeral solemnity. It appeared more like the internment of freedom than the anniversary of its birth. The countenances of the citizens generally appeared dejected, and the joy and festivity, which usually characterized the day, seemed to be superseded by sadness...The day was closed by the exhibition of a transparent painting with the figure of* John Jay *upon it. The figure was in full stature, dressed in a robe, holding in his right hand a pair of scales, containing in one scale* "American liberty and independence," *kicking the beam, in the other* "British gold" *in extreme preponderance; in his left hand a Treaty of Amity, Commerce and Navigation which he extended to a group of senators, who were grinning with pleasure and grasping at the Treaty. From the mouth of the figure*

issued these words contained in a label "Come up to my price and I will sell you my county." The procession began in Kensington and moved with great solemnity down Front Street to Callowhill Street, and down Second to Market-Street from thence to Front Street; and back again to Kensington. A great concourse of people attended the procession, and scarcely a whisper was heard until its return, when the shouts of repeated huzzas interrupted the solemnity of the scene. The figure was burned at Kensington amid the acclamation of hundreds of citizens.

What the reporter left out of the story was that the authorities did not take too kindly to the Kensingtonians' march. The militia was called out to break up the parade. A cavalry group, headed by Captain Morrell, was sent to Kensington but met resistance and was stoned. Writing to a friend, merchant Stephen Girard, a Jeffersonian, gave this account of the event:

We have had a demonstration here. The Kensington carpenters and certain other hot Republicans last Saturday formed a procession, carrying an effigy of that noble patriot, through the streets of our city, and ending by burning it at midnight on one of the heights of Kensington. I am told that everything went off very quietly, except that a few light horsemen were rolled in the mud and pelted with stones.

The crowds at Kensington numbered some five hundred citizens. The militia was overpowered and decided it best to retreat and let Kensington "continue its revels." It was said that the crowd commemorated its victory by erecting a signpost on the site of the encounter that read, "Morrel's Defeat—Jay Burned—July 4, 1795." Thus, Kensingtonians and Fishtowners' distaste for New Yorkers began.

BATCHELOR'S HALL REVISITED

In my first book, *Remembering Kensington and Fishtown*, I wrote a short piece about Batchelor's Hall. Since that time, much more research and even archaeological investigations have been conducted on this most ancient structure of Kensington. The following account gives a fuller history and shows the exact location of the hall, one of Kensington's most famous buildings.

By the nineteenth century, with Kensington growing, there was a petition taken up by citizens of the neighborhood to have Shackamaxon Street extended from Richmond Street (then called Queen) through to the Delaware River. People in the area began to complain that they had to go a full two squares out of their way to get to the riverfront, a route that greatly inconvenienced them, and since the area was not built up yet, it would be cheaper to cut a road through now (in 1816) than later, when perhaps development might have occurred.

Officials agreed, and Shackamaxon Street was cut through. Land surveys and illustrated road petition surveys show that Shackamaxon Street cut right through the old Batchelor's Hall property; however, the actual structure, burned in 1775 and built on top of, sat just south of the new piece of Shackamaxon Street and thus was not touched.

According to Benjamin Franklin scholar Professor Leo Lemay, Batchelor's Hall was "formed for fellowship and pleasure before 1728." If this is true, Batchelor's Hall not only predates the learned societies of the American Philosophical Society and the Library Company of Philadelphia but also is contemporary with Franklin's own Junto Club, which is said to have been founded in 1727.

Professor Lemay states that members of Batchelor's Hall were Franklin's friend Robert Grace, as well as Griffin Owen, Lloyd Zachary, Isaac Norris Jr. and Charles Norris. Philadelphia annalist John Fanning Watson adds Robert Charles, William Masters, John Sober and P. Graeme to the list. As well, George Webb, whom Franklin taught the art of printing, was a member. Some of these men were also in Franklin's Junto Club and were early members of those two other learned societies in Philadelphia previously mentioned.

It is due to George Webb that we know a lot of what little there is know about Batchelor's Hall. Webb penned a poem that celebrated Batchelor's Hall, and his mentor, Benjamin Franklin, printed it in 1731. It was appropriately titled "Bachelor's-Hall."

Batchelor's Hall had its share of luminaries visit the place. The hall would allow ministers from time to time to come and preach in Kensington, and according to a contemporary journal kept by a follower of the Moravian Church, on February 4, 1742, "Bro. Ludwig preached in Bachelor's Hall… with marked effect." Brother Ludwig is Nikolaus Ludwig von Zinzendorf (1700–1760), generally known as Count Zinzendorf, a German nobleman. He was the leader of the Moravian movement.

Later, in 1771, the Reverend John Murray, a Universalist minister, preached at Batchelor's Hall. Murray had been shut out from all the pulpits in Philadelphia but was welcomed by members of Batchelor's Hall. The place stood the customary "cannon shot" away from the city. Who would have thought that at such an early age Kensington was a place for liberal-minded men?

Another noted person who visited Batchelor's Hall was John Bartram (1699–1777), once called "the greatest natural botanist in the world." One source states that "the first botanic garden, for the cultivation of plants having medicinal properties, was established at Bachelor's Hall." It is quite possible that these plants were gathered from the local Native Americans and that even Bartram may have cared for this garden.

Batchelor's Hall is said to have been a square brick building. Since Paine Newman is known to have built his brick smith shop on top of the old foundation and his smith shop was thirty feet by seventy feet, then the hall, in all likelihood, was in the neighborhood of a thirty-foot-square structure. However, Torben Jenk suggests that the archaeological evidence revealed a foundation measuring eighteen feet wide on the river side with intact corners. He suspects that the building could have been L-shaped with a "piazza" looking south toward the bend in the Delaware, similar to the Fairman Mansion, which sat on the river at today's Penn Treaty Park, a block or so north of the hall.

The hall was said to have been of considerable beauty and was used chiefly for balls and late suppers. Watson's *Annals of Philadelphia* states that Batchelor's Hall "had a fine open view to the scenery on the Delaware." It stood on the east side of Hall Street, later Beach Street, still later Delaware Avenue, and sat 110 feet south of Shackamaxon, or within the now well-known historic area of the SugarHouse Casino site.

Christopher Marshall makes note in his diary on April 4, 1775, of the burning of the hall: "This morning a fire begun at nine o'clock, at Bachelor's Hall, which soon consumed the building." Other sources state that all the wooden portions were destroyed, which would seem to indicate that it was a brick building, as previously described, but perhaps had a wooden roof and interior.

Besides Webb's poem on the hall in its early years, the burning of Batchelor's Hall inspired several poems, one by Hopkinson and another by Thomas Paine (author of *Common Sense*) titled "Impromptu on Bachelor's Hall, at Philadelphia, being destroyed by Lightning, 1775."

Next to Fairman's Mansion, Batchelor's Hall was the most historic building in Kensington. But what happened to Batchelor's Hall after it was reported to burn down in 1775?

John Fanning Watson, the well-known Philadelphia antiquarian and annalist, states that a "brick smith shop" was built on the old foundation stones of the hall. The Kensington History Project (consisting of members Torben Jenk, Rich Remer and this author) contends that Paine Newman was the blacksmith who built his shop atop the old Batchelor's Hall and that the foundation of Batchelor's Hall sits within the SugarHouse Casino site.

However, SugarHouse's archaeological dig contends that Batchelor's Hall was not on the SugarHouse site but rather sat west of the property, somewhere between Richmond Street and Delaware Avenue. The three pieces of evidence used by SugarHouse to dismiss Batchelor's Hall from being on its property are a map of 1752, a newspaper advertisement of 1763 and a response to a "letter to the editor" of 1887.

In the 1752 Scull & Heap map, SugarHouse contended that the structure called "Hall" sitting on the west side of Richmond Street shows that the hall was not on its site. However, that piece of evidence would seem to contradict its second piece of evidence, an advertisement in the *Pennsylvania Gazette* of July 14, 1763, which states that a property on the west side of Richmond was for sale opposite Batchelor's Hall. "Opposite of Batchelor's Hall" would then seem to put Batchelor's Hall on the east side of Richmond Street, which contradicts the Scull & Heap map of 1752.

Batchelor's Hall was on the east side of Richmond Street, but the structure itself did not sit on Richmond Street. The "grounds" of the hall ran up to Richmond and down to the river; thus, saying the properties were "opposite" Batchelor's Hall simply means opposite the "Batchelor's Hall Grounds," which had a three-hundred-foot front on Richmond Street and ran down to the river.

The third piece of evidence for SugarHouse is from a response to an inquiry to the *Pennsylvania Magazine of History & Biography*, a journal of the Historical Society of Pennsylvania. Published in volume 11 of 1887, an inquirer asked where Batchelor's Hall was located, and the responder answered that it was located in the block bounded by Poplar, Shackamaxon, Beach and Allen Streets.

The person responding to the inquiry is not listed, nor is any source listed of where the responder found the information to support the assertion that

The uncovering of the foundation stones for Batchelor's Hall in 2008, east side of Delaware Avenue, 110 feet south of Shackamaxon Street. *Courtesy of Torben Jenk.*

Batchelor's Hall stood where he said it stood. Furthermore, the responder states that Batchelor's Hall stood on the block bounded by Poplar Street, Shackamaxon Street, Beach Street and Allen Street. This location is not a "block" but several blocks, as between Shackamaxon and Poplar Street in 1887 also ran Sarah Street, Frankford Avenue, Laurel Street and Lewellyn Street. If this letter responder shows anything, it seems to show that the author was not familiar with the geographic area he was talking about and did not even consult a map.

The Kensington History Project contended that Batchelor's Hall was on the SugarHouse site, and the evidence is in a survey of 1804 and in a road petition when Shackamaxon Street was cut through the grounds of the hall.

In 1804, Reading Howell, the official surveyor of Philadelphia, surveyed the "Batchelor's Hall Ground." The Batchelor's Hall ground is shown to run from the east side of Richmond Street to the low-water mark of the Delaware River and to have a front on Richmond Street of three hundred feet. On this survey is shown "Newman's Brick Smith Shop." The smith shop is shown to be on the east side of Hall Street (later changed to Beach, still later Delaware Avenue) and running eastward toward Penn Street. North of "Newman's Brick Smith Shop" is the portion of the Batchelor's Hall land that belonged to John Dickinson's family.

According to a contemporary road petition that was drawn up when Shackamaxon Street was cut through the Batchelor's Hall grounds, it was cut through that part of the grounds that was owned by Dickinson. Thus, "Newman's Brick Smith Shop" sat on the east side of Delaware Avenue, just south of Shackamaxon Street, squarely on the SugarHouse site.

Reading Howell's survey also shows no other "brick smith shop" on the Batchelor's Hall property. If one actually reads the historical record, it appears clear where Batchelor's Hall was located.

During the Kensington History Project's investigation into the history of the Point Pleasant area of Kensington (the Delaware River waterfront, south of Shackamaxon Street to Poplar Street), much information was revealed about Paine Newman, a colonial blacksmith whose brick smith shop is the one that Watson stated was built on the foundation of Batchelor's Hall.

On August 23, 1774, Paine Newman married Mary Coates, the daughter of a well-known Northern Liberties family (Fairmount Avenue was once known as Coates Street). Batchelor's Hall burned down several months after Paine Newman's marriage (April 4, 1775).

Tax lists and Provincial Council minutes show that during the Revolutionary War years, Paine Newman lived in Kensington's Point Pleasant area. In the "Minutes of the Provincial Council of Pennsylvania," dated September 28, 1776, Paine Newman was paid £6.8.6 for six anchors delivered to Captain Hazlewood. This shows him working at this time as a blacksmith, or shipsmith. On April 9, 1777, Paine Newman, with a Captain Miller and Jehu Eyre, were partners in the schooner *Dolphin*. Jehu Eyre and his brother-in-law Peter Browne, both of Kensington, built the schooner at Kensington. Various tax lists from 1779 to 1782 (proprietary, supply and state tax lists) all place Paine Newman as being located in the "Northern Liberties East Part," which was the designation for not only the Northern Liberties neighborhood of today but also for all of Kensington, including Point Pleasant. The 1780 tax list in particular shows Newman's occupation listed as "smith." He was listed in tax lists among the Coates and Browne families, all interlocked families known to be located near the Cohocksink Creek at Point Pleasant.

In 1783, Newman was one of the signers of the *Philadelphia Address to Congress*. On this list, he is sandwiched between George Lieb and Henry Brusstar (Brewster) and followed by William Masters, all from the Point Pleasant area. Henry Brusstar was the mastmaker whose wharf was at today's Shackamaxon Street. Lieb lived right at the bridge that went over the old Cohocksink Creek (Canal Street). Master's place was at Point Pleasant.

In October 1787, the *Independent Gazetteer* (October 3 and 20) ran an advertisement stating that Paine Newman had filed for bankruptcy. The *Pennsylvania Mercury* newspaper, dated November 16, 1787, shows Paine Newman's "Brick Smith's Shop" for sale. It states that the lot and ground was

> *situate, lying, and being in the township of the Northern Liberties and county of Philadelphia, containing in Front on Hall-Street 40 feet, and in length or depth 372 feet and a half to the river Delaware; bounded on the east by the river Delaware, on the west by land of Solomon Lyon, and on*

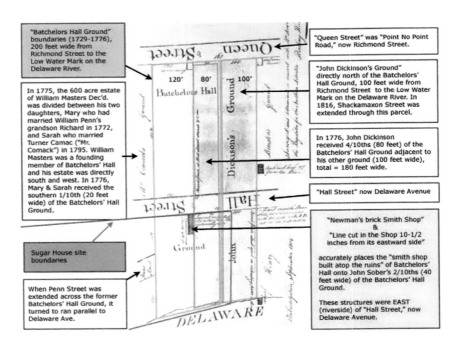

An 1804 Reading Howell Survey showing "Newman's brick Smith Shop" within the Batchelor's Hall Grounds, east side of Hall Street, later Delaware Avenue. *Courtesy of Torben Jenk.*

the north by ground of John Dickinson, Esq., and on the south by ground belonging to the heirs of William Allen, Esq., deceased; taken in execution as the property of Paine Newman, and to be sold by Joseph Cowperthwait, Sheriff. Philadelphia, Nov. 8, 1787.

This same "Brick Smith Shop" is shown on Reading Howell's survey of the "Batchelor's Hall Grounds" prepared in September 1804. Reading Howell (1743–1827) was a preeminent surveyor of Pennsylvania in his day, having been the Pennsylvania state surveyor as well as the surveyor for the city of Philadelphia.

There was no other "Brick Smith Shop" on the Batchelor's Hall Ground at this time (1775–1804). Reading Howell's 1804 survey clearly shows only one blacksmith on the Batchelor's Hall grounds, that being Paine Newman and his "brick smith shop." Research of the property deeds of all the lots laid out from the Batchelor's Hall grounds at the time in question also shows this to be true.

Collectively, this means that when the historian John Fanning Watson states that a brick smith shop was built upon the old foundation of Batchelor's Hall, he could only be speaking of Paine Newman. The Kensington History Project's research has clearly shown that Newman's brick smith shop was the smith shop built on the foundation of Batchelor's Hall, thus placing Batchelor's Hall squarely within the boundaries of the SugarHouse Casino site. Why this information was ignored by the Pennsylvania Historical Museum Commission is one of the oddest incidents in recent local history.

JOHN FANNING WATSON'S DESCRIPTION OF KENSINGTON

It might be difficult to picture, but the area where the Waterfront Square towers have now risen at Poplar Street and the Delaware River was once known as Point Pleasant. The peninsula-like piece of land lying between the old Cohocksink Creek (Canal Street) and the Delaware River was at one time a Kensington resort, surrounded on three sides by water: one side a creek, the other a bay and the third the river. The area had an inn, a distillery, a tavern and opportunities for sport shooting.

John Watson tells us in his *Annals of Philadelphia* (1830) that the Delaware River formerly made a great inroad upon the land at the mouth of the

Cohocksink Creek (Poplar Street and the Delaware River) "making there a large and shallow bay, extending from Point Pleasant down to Warder's long wharf, near Green Street," and that back in the 1790s the water used to come up daily to the houses at Front and Coates (Fairmount) Streets. All the area of the bay (then without the present streets east of Front Street) was "an immense plane of spatterdocks, a common North American water lily, which filled the bay from the end of Warder's wharf at Green Street and on a line with Point Pleasant."

Watson also mentions:

> *The lower end of Coates' Street was then lower than now; and in freshets the river laid across Front Street. All the ten or twelve houses north of Coates' Street, on the east side, were built on made ground, and their little yards were supported with wharf logs, and bush willows as trees. [At] the then mouth of [the] Cohocksink was a wooden drawbridge, then the only communication to Kensington, which crossed at Leib's house opposite to Poplar Lane; from thence a raised causeway ran across to*

Archibald Robinson's *View of Philadelphia* (1777) across the Cohocksink Creek, showing, at left, some of the old structures at Point Pleasant, Kensington. *Courtesy of Torben Jenk.*

Point Pleasant. The stone bridge north of it [at Front Street] *leading to Kensington was not then in existence. On the outside of this causeway the river covered, and spatterdocks grew, and on the inside there was a great extent of marshy ground alternately wet and dry, with the ebbing and flowing of the tide; the creek was embanked on the east side. The marsh was probably two hundred feet wide where the causeway at the stone bridge now runs…The marsh grounds of Cohocksink used to afford good shooting for woodcock and snipe, &c.*

One of the earliest advertisements for Point Pleasant is by William Masters, on August 1, 1765, when he states that at the last day of that month, he would be selling a large, three-story brick house on Germantown Road, at the upper end of Second Street and if a person were interested, he could contact Masters at his distillery at "Point Pleasant, near Kensington." Masters was a fairly large landowner in the area, owning at one time most of Point Pleasant. His lands stretched north and west to Girard Avenue and beyond.

Another business advertisement for Point Pleasant is from May 24, 1770, when an advertisement in the *Pennsylvania Gazette* is printed for Elizabeth Phillips's cured sturgeon. She was advertised as being next to William Masters's distillery and would appear to be one of the earliest mentions of a female fishmonger in the area that would later be called Fishtown. Phillips was again advertising her kegs of cured sturgeon, done in the "Baltick manner," in the *Pennsylvania Gazette* on April 30, 1772. There was also in 1771 an advertisement for "an assortment of ironmongery and sundry other articles" at the house of Thomas Savadge, at Point Pleasant, in the Northern Liberties of the city of Philadelphia, near Kensington.

With these developments and early businesses, Point Pleasant became the "downtown" area of Kensington. Point Pleasant had shipyards within it, and by 1820, the Point Pleasant Fire Company was founded and located on the Delaware River at the mouth of the Cohocksink Creek. There was also the earliest post office in Kensington founded at Point Pleasant, and the Kensington National Bank was founded on Beach Street in 1826.

The area of Point Pleasant used to be elevated somewhat, and during the American Revolution, the British put an artillery unit there and it became known as Artillery Hill. It helped the British to defend Philadelphia from the Americans who might try coming down the Delaware River from the north. The Brits also dammed the Cohocksink Creek, flooding the

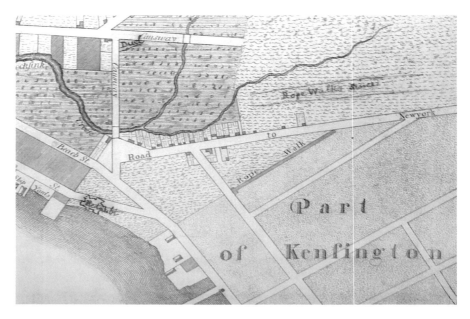

Davies 1794 map showing Kensington development, as well as British Redoubt No. 1 drawn in by the annalist, John Fanning Watson. *Courtesy of Torben Jenk.*

marshes even more, which helped their defenses on the northern end of the city. After the war, and as the area went under further development, Artillery Hill was leveled and the dirt was used to fill in the marshes and the spatterdock-filled bay.

With all of the development going on in this area of Kensington today, with the building of SugarHouse Casino and the Waterfront Towers, it looks like Point Pleasant will soon again be a resort of sorts. Who says history doesn't repeat itself?

CHAPTER 2
Industry and Labor

THE JOHNSON BROTHERS AND FREDERICK SANNO, EARLY KENSINGTON STEAM ENGINE BUILDERS

Historians tell us of John Fitch, Robert Fulton and Oliver Evans and their early experiments with steam engines. The first successful launching of a steamboat, John Fitch's *Perseverance*, took place on July 20, 1786, years before the more popularly known launch of Robert Fulton's *Clermont*. Fitch's experiment took place at a shipyard at Kensington's Point Pleasant. Oliver Evans, the famed inventor of the first steam-propelled carriage in the world, experimented with his invention right here in Philadelphia as well. However, Evans failed to get his steam carriage into use and died in 1819. Other, lesser-known steam engine builders known to historians also worked out of Kensington's Point Pleasant area, an area that became well known as an incubator for the Industrial Revolution.

John Watson tells us in his *Annals of Philadelphia* (1879) that a steam carriage, built by Nicholas and James Johnson in Kensington, was run upon the streets of Kensington in 1827–28. This experiment was quite early, as Peter Cooper's Tom Thumb, considered to be the first American-built steam locomotive to be operated on a common-carrier railroad, was built a couple of years later in 1830.

In a work by Joseph Harrison titled *The Locomotive Engine, and Philadelphia's Share in its Early Improvements* (1872), we find that the Johnson brothers had a

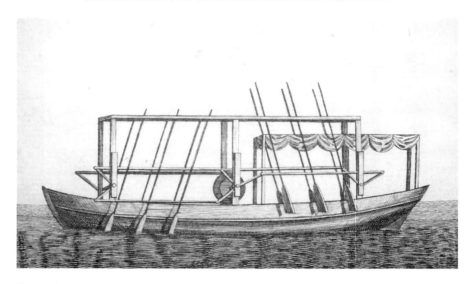

Illustration of John Fitch's design for a ferryboat with steam-driven oars, taken from the *Columbian Magazine*, December 8, 1786. *Courtesy of Torben Jenk.*

small engineering firm on Penn Street in the old district of Kensington, just above the Cohocksink Creek, the southern border of Kensington.

An eyewitness to the Johnsons' experiment saw it under construction when it made several trial runs through the streets of Kensington. The eyewitness described it as being a "crudely constructed machine." It had "but a single cylinder, set horizontally, with connecting-rod attachments to a single crank at the middle of the driving axle. Its two driving wheels were made of wood, the same as an ordinary road wagon, and were of large diameter, certainly not less than eight feet. It had two smaller wheels in front, arranged in the usual manner of an ordinary road wagon for guiding the movement of the machine. It had an upright boiler hung on behind, shaped like a huge bottle, the smoke-pipe coming out through the center at top, formed the neck of the bottle."

Its initial trial runs were rather comical and were made on the unpaved roads in the immediate area of the Johnsons' shop on Penn Street. The machine showed an evident "lack of boiler as well as cylinder power"; however, it did "run continuously for some time and surmount considerable elevations in the roads." The safety value was held down by a weight and lever, and it was said to be "somewhat amusing to see the puff, puff, puff, of the safety valve as the machine jolted over the rough street."

The engine was sometimes unmanageable in its steering. On what became its final trial run while it was crossing the High Bridge (which lay over the Cohocksink Creek) and turning onto Brown Street, the driver was unable to turn quick enough and it jumped the curb, smashing into the awning posts and window of a house at the southwest corner of Brown and Oak Streets. Oak Street later became Beach Street; the High Bridge was an extension of Oak (Beach) Street that crossed over the Cohocksink Creek, becoming Beach Street in Kensington (the creek being the historical border between Kensington and the Northern Liberties). The Johnsons' shop was just north of the High Bridge, on Penn Street, which is the small sliver of street fronting the new Waterfront Square high-rise towers on the river.

After the steam carriage struck the house on Brown and Oak Streets, the Johnsons' engine was not seen on the streets of Kensington again, nor is it known what became of the machine and its makers.

Information on who the Johnson brothers were remains a mystery. The 1820 census shows us they were in Kensington by at least that year. Nicholas Johnson's household was made up of him, his wife, a daughter and one other female, possibly a servant or sibling. James Johnson's household had him, his wife and one other male, again perhaps a servant, boarder or even an employee or sibling. Both households were listed as having one person in manufacturing, so it would appear that the brothers were in business by 1820. In 1820, they were enumerated along the waterfront in Kensington's Point Pleasant area, where their shop was located.

Nicholas and James Johnson were still in Kensington in 1830, as witnessed by the census of that year. By 1830, both men's families had grown to about half a dozen or so children each. While Nicholas Johnson doesn't show up in the 1840 census for Kensington, there is a James Johnson as late as 1850 in the general riverfront area, listed as a manufacturer. Further research would have to be conducted to see what became of these Johnson brothers and if they are the Nicholas and James Johnson who are recorded as having immigrated to Philadelphia in 1809. If the 1850 census record for the Kensington James Johnson who was a manufacturer is correct, the brothers may have been from Ireland.

Besides the Johnson brothers at Point Pleasant, the area of Kensington that sat between the winding Cohocksink Creek and the Delaware River, there was another early steam engine builder named Frederick D. Sanno. Sanno, also seen as Frederick DeSanno, is stated to have been born

October 17, 1780. He was the son of Charles Beraud DeSanno (b. May 31, 1746) of Luxembourg, France. Frederick first married Hanna at Red Hill, Montgomery County, Pennsylvania. That marriage did not last; they divorced, and he remarried to Sarah Bickley Heaton on October 10, 1815, in Camden, New Jersey. Sarah was the daughter of William and Mary Heaton.

Sanno is found listed in the *Philadelphia Directory & Stranger's Guide for 1825* as "Frederick D. Sanno, brass founder, Penn near Marsh (K)." This address is today's Penn Street near Poplar (Marsh) Street in (K)ensington. He would have been located alongside the above-mentioned Johnson brothers.

While listed as a brass founder, Sanno also experimented in steam engines. While located at Kensington, he employed as an apprentice the soon-to-be-famous Joseph Harrison Jr., who came to Sanno to learn steam engineering at the age of fifteen. Sanno's business failed after two years (1825–26), and Harrison left to apprentice under James Flint of Hyde & Flint (Soho Works). Harrison later worked for Philip Garrett, Arundus Tiers and William Norris, all the while learning steam engineering and locomotive building. He eventually became a partner in Garrett, Eastwick, & Co. After Garrett died, the company came to be known as Eastwick & Harrison. The company was so well established that Harrison contracted with the Czar of Russia to build the St. Petersburg and Moscow Railway, a $3 million contract, from 1843 to 1848. When Harrison returned to America, he built his mansion on Rittenhouse Square and bought at auction in England Benjamin West's original painting of *Penn's Treaty with the Indians*, bringing the famous painting back to Philadelphia. It eventually wound up in the collections of the Pennsylvania Academy of Art, where it hangs today.

After Sanno's business failed at Point Pleasant, he is thought to have gone back to his wife's family in Montgomery County and continued to follow his mechanical inclinations. A property deed executed in Montgomery County for October 22, 1832, involves Sanno, his wife and her parents. It was recorded April 3, 1835.

On August 16, 1836, Sanno contracted to be a master mechanic to superintend the Norris Locomotive Works at Bush Hill, Parkesburg, Chester County, Pennsylvania. Sanno built locomotives in the great Norris Locomotive Works in Norristown, Pennsylvania. It is there that he laid down the Victoria, the first locomotive built in America for England.

Sanno is found in the 1840 Philadelphia City Directory listed as "DeSanno, Frederick, machinist, NE Noble & Franklin." An application for a patent was submitted by Frederick D. Sanno, of the county of Chester and state of Pennsylvania, on April 15, 1841. He stated to have "invented a method for repairing and renewing old and worn out brass boxes for machinery & more particularly Locomotive Steam Engines & Rail Road Cars."

From 1844 to 1846, the time of his death, his home was at Coates (Fairmount) Street above Thirteenth, and his title was that of engineer. Though he maintained his residence in Philadelphia, he was under contract with Norris for a period of three years and may not have lived there all that much.

Frederick died at his home, 527 Coates Street, Philadelphia, of "brain disease." A copy of his obituary reads, "On Wednesday evening, 6th, Mr. Frederick De Sanno, machinist, in the 66th year of his age. His friends and acquaintances, and those of the family and also the members of the Charles Carroll and Workingmen's Societies, are respectfully invited to attend his funeral, on Sunday afternoon, at 3 o'clock, without further notice, from his late residence, No. 527 Coates Street below Broad."

Frederick D. Sanno was buried in Lot no. 244, Section A, 4 North, in Monument Cemetery, which used to be located at Broad and Berks Streets in Philadelphia. Sarah, Frederick's wife, continued to reside in the family home until her death. She was buried beside her husband as well as a number of other Sanno family members. Today, the cemetery is long closed, the Sanno family bodies have been removed and the old cemetery is part of Temple University's campus. The bodies of the DeSanno family were moved to Lawnview Cemetery at Rockledge, Pennsylvania. A simple bronze marker "DeSanno" marks the graves.

JOHN BROMLEY & SONS, CARPET WEAVERS

One of the more curious coincidences I've encountered over the years while studying Kensington's history is the fact that the site of one of America's greatest textile mills, John Bromley & Sons at B Street and Lehigh Avenue, was replaced by a welfare office. This coincidence pretty much sums up the state of post-industrial America.

Philip Scranton's "Build a Firm, Start Another: The Bromleys and Family Firm Entrepreneurship in the Philadelphia Region" (*Business History* 35, no. 4, October 1993) contains an interesting history of this iconic Kensington textile mill family.

Portrait of John Bromley (1800–1883), patriarch of the Bromley family's many textile mills, an empire that lasted over 145 years and five generations.

The Bromley family's textile business has a more than 145-year history that expanded over five generations. Those old enough to remember Bromley's probably don't recall much of the early history of the company, so I'll amuse the reader with this little history of those early years.

John Bromley was born in 1800, the son of a wool weaver from a small town in Yorkshire, England, named Hanging Heaton. Bromley grew up in the textile business working with his father. When he married at the age of twenty-seven, John began working on his own as a handloom weaver. With his father and others, he started a carding mill at Batley Carr, in Yorkshire.

Bromley fathered five sons and two daughters with his wife: George (1828), James (1829), Mary (1831), Ellen (1833), Thomas (1835), Charles (circa 1836–1838) and Edward (circa 1839–1840).

Looking for greater opportunities, he immigrated to Philadelphia in 1841. He found work in New Jersey at a woolen spinning mill, where he was abruptly struck with not only the death of his son Edward but also the death of his wife. By 1843, he remarried to a woman by the name of Lucinda Smalley.

After the New Jersey spinning mill failed, Bromley moved back to Philadelphia, where he took up carpet weaving in 1845. In 1847, he was found in Kensington, in a rented room at Fifth Street and Germantown

One of the original buildings of John Bromley & Sons mills, Front and Jasper Streets. The family located in this area of Kensington by 1860.

Avenue, listed as a manufacturer of carpets. By the year 1860, Bromley had bought an unused dye house at York and Jasper Streets and soon filled it with over three dozen handlooms. His American textile operations were underway.

With his new wife, Lucinda, Bromley fathered five other children: John H. (circa 1845), Phoebe, Anne, Joseph H. (1861) and Edward (circa 1862).

Coming from a Quaker background, Bromley was able to use his religious affiliation at the local meetinghouses to help network with the old Quaker City's merchants, which helped his fledgling carpet business.

As the Civil War approached, Bromley was running a textile factory with his three older sons from his first marriage. After the war was over, Bromley helped these three sons start their own business. In 1868, Bromley Brothers (George, James and Thomas) was founded. Bromley's three sons from his second wife (John H., Joseph H. and Edward) all worked for their father's firm and eventually became partners of that business. The new name of the firm was John Bromley & Sons.

The Bromley Brothers mill was located across the street from their father's original mill at York and Jasper Streets. It was four stories and contained twelve thousand square feet. About the year 1878, the mill burned down, forcing the brothers to rent space at a nearby factory. Within the year, they reopened a five-story factory filled with a one-hundred-horsepower engine that powered 120 looms. They also built their own dye house. They soon employed just as many workers as Bromley & Sons, specializing in "ingrain, Venetian and 'patent Imperial Damask carpets.'"

In 1875, Bromley and Sons employed about two hundred people, with about fifty of them being women. At about this time, he introduced power carpet looms alongside his handlooms.

By the early 1880s, the Bromley family's companies, Bromley & Sons and Bromley Brothers, became major players in the carpet industry. When John Bromley's sons took over Bromley & Sons, they began moving out of the "flat ingrains" carpet market and producing more "pile Brussels carpeting." They also began producing Smyrna carpeting, which differed from ingrain and Brussels. Bromley Brothers continued to produce damasks and Venetians.

Bromley Brothers dissolved its partnership in 1881. Thomas Bromley kept the company name and founded a mill in the same area of the neighborhood. Brothers George and James kept control of the factory. Thomas went on to employ about 350 workers by 1882, producing "Wilton, Brussels, Ingrain, and Venetian Carpets." George and James reopened as the Albion Mill at the same location (northeast corner of Hagert and Jasper Streets), employing some 305 workers at 140 looms.

In 1883, John Bromley, the patriarch of the family died. By 1885, Bromley & Sons, now run by John Bromley's sons from his second wife (John H., Joseph & Edward) stopped producing ingrain carpeting and filled their factory with handlooms for producing Smyrnas.

James Bromley died in 1885, and his brother George continued producing ingrains at the Albion Mill for the rest of his career. Meanwhile, John H., Joseph and Edward expanded John Bromley & Sons and increased the amount of looms by 100 percent, running 650 looms and becoming the largest handloom business in the country by the year 1890. They were the largest employer of handloom weavers in the United States, employing over 750 weavers.

In 1888, John Bromley & Sons founded the Bromley Manufacturing Company (BMC) for the production of curtains and upholstery fabrics. This new factory was situated near the brothers' carpet mill. They soon added a second facility a couple of blocks north.

While the Bromley brothers prospered, they also created families. Four of the brothers had families of their own, which produced at least ten sons, all of whom joined the family business, making it the third generation to run the various Bromley mills.

During and before the 1880s, most of the Bromley brothers lived in Kensington, either along York Street near the factories or in the large houses that used to line Cumberland Street east of Kensington Avenue. Some lived on Norris Square, which at that time was a rather fashionable neighborhood with large town houses surrounding the square. By the 1890s, as the family prospered, they began to move to the "new money" neighborhood of North Broad Street, above Girard, a place where many Kensington manufacturers moved to once they became wealthy.

George Bromley died in 1902. His son James and son-in-law James Birch took over Albion Mills, dividing it in order to bring in family members, but they went out of business by 1912. Thomas Bromley continued on, incorporating in 1891, bringing in his sons in the mid-1890s and buying out the other investors. However, once Thomas died about 1902, his son and namesake, Thomas Jr., bought out his brothers, and it became clear very quickly that the younger Thomas was unable to run the business successfully. He was out of business by 1906, thus ending the three elder sons' textile history.

While the older brothers' businesses were failing, the three younger brothers were operating eight different and very successful textile companies: Bromley & Sons, Smyrna & Axminster (carpets), BMC (lace curtains and upholsteries), National Lace (owned by Bromley & Sons), Joseph H. Bromley (lace), Lehigh Manufacturing (lace curtains), North American Lace and Glenwood Lace Mills. Most of these factories were in Kensington, or just west of Kensington, around Twenty-second Street and Lehigh Avenue.

By 1907, the Bromleys merged North American and Glenwood, and in 1911, Joseph H. Bromley merged his namesake company with Lehigh Manufacturing, creating the new brand name of Quaker Lace, located at Fourth and Lehigh Streets. By 1913, the number of employees had grown to over four thousand.

The nation's largest carpet mill (eleven acres of floor space), built by the Bromley family on Lehigh Avenue between Front and B Streets, circa 1889–92.

John Bromley & Sons' crowning achievement was its large five-story power loom mill, which was built along Lehigh Avenue between B and Gurney Streets between 1889 and 1892 (Gurney Street is now vacated) to at first house the Bromley Manufacturing Company but later Bromley & Sons as well. This structure, opposite the Episcopal Hospital, covered a full square block and ran back to Somerset Street. It contained over eleven acres of floor space and employed about 2,300 people. It was described in 1894 as "undoubtedly the largest of [its] kind in the world."

In addition to the main building of the factory, the complex included a "picker house, office building, wing buildings, lace mill, chenille mill, weave shed, dye house, boiler house, engine house, sizing house, and cop boiling house." From this mill, the company manufactured "chenille curtains and table covers, and lace curtains in a great variety of artistic designs." The mill was equipped with over one thousand looms.

Looking back to the 1880s, the Bromley family had become one of the major players in the U.S. carpet industry. They continued to expand, and at one point the family (father and six sons) had built and run at least ten different textile mills, producing all sorts of carpets, lace and other products. As the three older brothers aged and died, they did not produce offspring to run their businesses successfully, and those companies folded. However, the three younger brothers prospered by adapting to the new technology and finding niche markets. They controlled eight separate factories at one point before merging four of them into two.

In 1912, Quaker Lace (a company formed by the merger of two of the Bromleys' lace firms) began direct-mail advertising to clients and retailers and opened a large showroom in Manhattan. By 1913, the Bromleys employed over four thousand workers. Their annual sales were upward of $10 million.

World War I did not stifle the running of the Bromley Empire. The workforce dipped to three thousand, but the company still came through the war in good shape. By this time, a third generation of Bromleys began to be brought into the family business: the sons of Joseph H. Bromley (Charles, Henry, John and Joseph Jr.). However, by the 1920s, fashion was changing, and the "great lace boom" was starting to fade as styles and trends changed. The Bromleys controlled 30 percent of the lace market in the United States, and with lace going out of fashion, a new product was needed.

The third generation (except Joseph Jr., who stayed with Quaker Lace) of Bromleys found silk hosiery to be their new product and in 1919 founded Quaker Hosiery Company, which they set up in their Quaker Lace building. Like they did with lace, they marketed their hosiery directly to retailers. In 1927, the silk hosiery business was so profitable that the Bromley sons saw annual salaries of upward of $93,000 each (equivalent to $2 million today).

An accounting of the Bromley family in the late 1920s, before the 1929 stock market crash, showed Joseph Bromley's North American and Quaker Lace firms employing almost 1,100 workers. John E. Bromley, who took over the carpet aspect of the business (Bromley & Sons, Bromley Manufacturing Co.) from William H. Bromley, employed about 1,500 employees. The new enterprise of silk hosiery employed just over 700 workers, for a family total of about 3,300 employees.

The 1930s were a period of difficulties for the Bromley family as the second generation gave way to the third and fourth generations. Joseph H. Bromley, a son of the founder John Bromley, died in 1931. He left an estate worth $6.5 million. The Great Depression hit the Bromley mills, and like many others, their workforce dropped greatly, with over one thousand losing their jobs.

It was also in the 1930s that a fourth-generation Bromley, Charles Bromley Jr., was brought in to be the treasurer of Quaker Hosiery by his father. Another fourth-generation Bromley, the son of John E. Bromley, was brought in by his father to be the treasurer of the original John Bromley & Sons mill on Lehigh Avenue. The newer generation hoped to bring Bromley in line with the leaders in the silk hosiery industry. They purchased some smaller firms and reached the production of the nation's leader (Gotham and Berkshire). However, by 1937, their four hosiery mills folded.

Fortunes for the fourth generation of Bromleys were not as great as earlier generations. As each decade passed, the factories' workforce shrunk. From 1945 employment levels of 1,119 at the four remaining mills, the numbers decreased to 348 in 1963 at the surviving three companies. The production of textiles at nonunion shops in the South and overseas were the final nails in the Bromley coffin.

Quaker Lace hung on through the 1980s, with a fifth-generation Bromley running the last of the Bromley mills. In 1992, this business finally closed, ending five generations and 145 years of a Kensington textile family.

The site today of the Lehigh Avenue Bromley & Sons mill. It is a stark contrast from the world's largest carpet mill to a government-run welfare office.

John Bromley & Sons, on Lehigh Avenue, across from Episcopal Hospital, closed in the early 1960s. A fire in the 1970s was the final demise of the world's largest carpet mill. Today a welfare office and a social service agency have replaced it, giving one the picture of what life has become for working-class people in postindustrial America.

H.W. Butterworth, Hero Fruit Jar Company and the Founding of the Riverfront Railroad Spur

A couple of months back I sat on my step on a Friday night watching people walk by. For a moment I thought I was down the shore on a summer night watching the parade of people on the boardwalk; there were that many people. I realize it's not an unusual occurrence on a busy street like York, but the people coming and going were almost exclusively the newer residents in the neighborhood. They were all heading toward an art opening at 2424 East York Street, a new invention of what used to be the Jacob Holtz factory.

The old Jacob Holtz factory, previously the H.W. Butterworth building, reincarnated yet again into the office building known as 2424 East York Street.

The old factory has been converted into office space for the designer class, with an immense atrium gallery space in the center of the building complex that usually has an art exhibition on display. Most of the original interior has been saved and offices built out with hardwood floors, exposed brick walls and high ceilings. A number of tenants have already taken up space, with more to join in the near future.

Friends and family of mine worked at Jacob Holtz. It wasn't that pleasant smelling if you worked there; the smell of plastics could be overwhelming. Holtz was a Russian immigrant who came to Philadelphia in about 1910 when he was only ten years old. His father was a cobbler. About 1949, with his son-in-law Zeldan Rentz, they started a business on Germantown Avenue, calling it Jacob Holtz Company. They fabricated tubing for the furniture industry. After moving a couple of times to Huntingdon Park and Port Richmond, they eventually acquired the old H.W. Butterworth & Sons building, at today's present 2424 East York Street location. They expanded and moved their business to Kensington (Fishtown) in 1970.

The company did quite well and became one of the leaders of its field, making all sorts of casters used by the furniture industry. After Jacob Holtz retired, his son-in-law ran the company. After his death, it was taken over by his son David in 1986. David Rentz sold the company in 1999.

The new owners bought out an Illinois-based company and moved it to Fishtown. They were one of only three companies in America that manufactured casters. Eventually they moved to a newer facility at Lester, Pennsylvania, outside of Philadelphia and sold the building to the present owners.

H.W. Butterworth & Sons, manufacturers of machinery for the textile industry, originally constructed the factory complex on York Street. The original Butterworth was John Butterworth, who immigrated to America from England sometime in the early nineteenth century. By 1820, he had established himself in the Northern Liberties and was listed as having a business in "tin work" for cotton and woolen machinery. He was located on Second Street, north of Brown. The family lived in Northern Liberties at first, but like many Kensington manufacturers, they moved to the "new money" neighborhood of North Broad Street after they became successful.

After John's death, his son Henry Whitaker Butterworth took over the business and moved the plant from Second Street to Haydock Street, east of Front. After constructing a new factory at York and Cedar Streets, he moved the factory there by at least 1870. Between 1870 and 1884, the company continued to expand, enlarging its facilities and eventually buying up the old American Hot Cast Porcelain Works that sat across from it on York Street. This was the building complex where the Catholic printing company Jeffries & Manz was located before moving. Almost an entire block of new homes now occupies this site.

Between 1867 and 1908, Butterworth & Sons showed its ingenuity by filing for a number of patents on various improvements on steam drying cylinders, tentering and mercerizing machines, automatic clamps for cloth-stretching machines and improvements on calendaring rolls and vacuum values.

In 1889, after bringing in all three of his sons, the company was incorporated as H.W. Butterworth & Sons Co., builders of bleaching, dyeing, drying and finishing machinery. The officers of the company were James Butterworth, president; Charles C. Butterworth, vice-president; William B. Butterworth, treasurer; and Harry W. Butterworth, secretary.

H.W. Butterworth & Sons was a company that lasted over one hundred years with only family at the helm managing it. Powers & Company, Inc. is presently involved with trying to list the H.W. Butterworth & Sons Company Building on the National Register of Historic Places.

About the year 1884, a railroad line was run from Richmond Street west on Lehigh Avenue to Cedar Street and then south on Cedar to Commerce (Moyer) Street and south on Commerce to York Street, where it turned west and went over York to Cedar Street. The rail line had branches that ran off York up Gaul and Almond Streets to those manufacturers on those streets, including a connection with the machine works of H.W. Butterworth & Sons. These tracks were a spur that connected with the Riverfront Railroad and the Philadelphia and Reading Railroad Company. The Riverfront Railroad ran along the Delaware Riverfront, along today's Richmond Street and Delaware Avenue. This author remembers as a youth some of these boxcars traveling over York Street and going into the Jacob Holtz building.

Another local company that was instrumental in getting this Riverfront Railroad Spur to loop through the neighborhood was the Hero Fruit Jar Company, which, with Butterworth, was the main sponsor of the rail line.

Two companies dominated the canning jar industry during the period from 1860 to 1890: Consolidated Fruit Jar Company of New York and the Hero Fruit Jar Company of Philadelphia. Hero was founded just after the Civil War by Salmon B. Rowley (1827–1905) a native New Yorker. His jars

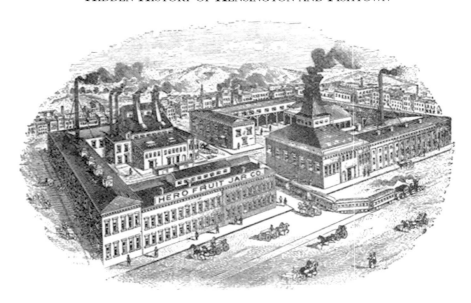

The original buildings of Hero Fruit Jar Company, once the country's leader in the canning jar field, located between Hagert, Letterly, Almond and Cedar Streets.

were distinguished by a "Hero Cross" on them, a reference to the heroes of the Civil War. The cross looked similar to the Iron Cross but had the initials of H, F, J and Co. Today, some of these jars can bring good money in the bottle-collecting world.

One of Rowley's inventions was a specialized lid design for the jars "consisting of a top-sealing jar with a metal or glass lid straddling the ground lip, held down by a zinc band." In an era when many families canned their own food, these preserving jars were extremely important and popular, and Rowley sold them throughout the country.

The most well-known canning jar today is still the Mason jar, developed by John L. Mason about 1858. Rowley's glass insert came about in 1868, and with the screw lids and lid liners, it helped decrease the chances of spoilage. Rowley battled in the courts throughout the last half of the nineteenth century against patent infringements on his inventions and was also taken to court in 1869 by Mason himself for the same charges, but the court found in Rowley's favor.

Trying to keep up with the competition, Rowley overextended himself and became $150,000 in debt by 1879. This was remedied with the help of the Kennedy family, who controlled the Spring Garden Bank. Rowley's daughter had married into the Kennedy clan. The bank cheaply bought

A canning jar produced by the Hero Fruit Jar Company, showing its trademark "Iron Cross" and the company's initial, "H. F.J. & Co."

Rowley's Hero Glass Works at a sheriff's sale, incorporated it under the name of the Hero Fruit Jar Company and appointed Rowley as president. Several Kennedy family members acted as the other officers, and the bank spent money on improvements to the company.

This model worked well for a while, and the company was very profitable throughout the 1880s, when it passed Consolidated as the leading fruit jar maker in America. However, by the early 1890s, when its patents had expired and payouts were reduced, it became a burden on Spring Garden Bank, which still held the mortgage. With other similar investments, the bank eventually collapsed in 1891.

Losing out on its most favored lender, the Hero Fruit Jar Company stumbled along until Salmon B. Rowley died in 1905. By 1909, the company had become the Hero Manufacturing Company and no longer made glass jars, becoming sheet metal specialists instead. Over time, the complex at

Recently vacated by the Joseph P. Cattie Galvanizing & Tinning Works, this original building of the Hero Fruit Jar Company is abandoned, waiting for development.

Gaul and Hagert Streets was taken over by the Joseph P. Cattie Galvanizing & Tinning Works, which in turn was bought out by the German firm Voight & Schweitzer. Only recently was it closed by the company. The two-block site now sits vacant.

In its early years, Hero manufactured chiefly glass fruit jars. In 1869–70, the glassworks started out within the block where the old Cattie Galvanizing building stands today (Gaul and Almond and Letterly and Hagert Streets). By 1874, it had expanded and occupied almost the entire block between Gaul and Cedar and Hagert and Letterly Streets (except the row of houses that still sit on Cedar Street). This expanded lot of the company is today's large empty lot with the cinder block wall around it.

At this time (1870), there were no houses built on the adjacent blocks. Within a year, all the wooden frame buildings were taken down and rebuilt in brick, including the "new glass house" on the west side of Gaul Street where the company had additional ovens and smelting furnaces and several long wooden frame storage facilities for finished products.

By 1889, Hero was listed as having 750 workers when in full operation (150 girls, 300 boys, balance men). After the company's incorporation, it expanded its products. Besides the manufacture of Mason-improved glass jars and trimmings, it also produced all kinds of sheet and white metal, nickel, silver and gold-plated goods.

As previously noted, H.W. Butterworth & Sons and the Hero Fruit Jar Company were the two main businesses that backed the laying out of the Riverfront Railroad spur down York Street. This spur of the Riverfront Railroad became a reality in 1883 and allowed these local manufactories of today's Thirty-first Ward to be connected not only by rail to the Philadelphia waterfront but also to the whole rail system of the Philadelphia & Reading Railroad, Pennsylvania Railroad and the B&O Railroad lines and, by extension, to other major railroad lines that ran throughout the country.

The rail spur actually started out coming west on Lehigh Avenue from Richmond Street. The Riverfront Railroad ran along Richmond Street, Beach Street and Delaware Avenue, connecting by rail all the manufactories along Philadelphia's waterfront. In the Kensington and Fishtown area of the city, as the blocks west of the Delaware River saw the development of manufacturing establishments, there was a need to run a spur of the Riverfront Railroad into the residential sections of the neighborhood, where some factories had set up business during the period between the end of the Civil War (1865) and the early 1880s.

As could be expected, the idea of running railroad tracks through residential streets was hotly contested by Kensington's residents. Back in the 1830s, an all-out riot ensued when rail lines were attempted to be laid down along Front Street above Girard. The opposition at that time won the battle; this time it would not.

This time the opponents to the railway rallied around an assistant pastor from St. Anne's Church (Cedar Street and Lehigh Avenue), whose school was said to have had one thousand students at that time. The train line would have the tracks laid practically outside the school's front doors, and the fear was that children would be killed crossing the tracks. Deaths from railroad crossings were a common occurrence in nineteenth-century Philadelphia. It was the main reason why the trains were eventually elevated in the 1910s, forcing those houses along Lehigh Avenue (and the side streets for a block) to construct a flight of stairs to get into their front doors. This was due to the excavation of the roads so the trains would not have to be elevated so high.

While members of the community protested, this time they did not have the support of local businessmen. The local businesses and, presumably, thousands of their employees who lived in the area all supported the rail line, as it meant better profits and more work due to the efficiency of shipping and receiving of raw and finished goods. The protesters filed a lawsuit against the railroad, but the judge dismissed their claims, and the railroad was built.

The rail tracks were laid down on Lehigh Avenue west from Richmond Street, crossing the old Aramingo Canal, turning south onto Cedar Street and then immediately onto Moyer Street, running all the way down Moyer Street to York Street, turning west on York Street and ending at Cedar Street.

During this time, Moyer Street was named Commerce Street, and it ran through from Lehigh to York. Moyer Street acted as the ground road for the various businesses that lined the Aramingo Canal—hence "Commerce" Street. Aramingo Avenue would have been a better route and wider, but since it was still a canal and would not be converted into a street until the end of the 1890s, Moyer Street served the purpose. Train tracks along Moyer Street can still be seen between Cumberland and York.

Along this branch there were mini spurs of the line that ran into a number of local manufactories, including the previously discussed H.W. Butterworth & Sons on both sides of York Street, between Cedar and Gaul Streets, and Hero Fruit Jar Company, which was located on the two blocks between Hagert and Letterly and Almond and Cedar Streets.

John T. Lewis, an old lead works (later Dutch Boy Paints, still later Anzon Lead), was connected to the railroad from Commerce Street. This company originally started out on the east side of the Aramingo Canal, from Cumberland to Huntingdon (where Applebees, Wawa and Rite Aid now are). Once the canal was turned into a street, it expanded across Aramingo Avenue. A rail spur at about Firth and Moyer Streets entered the western plant of John T. Lewis and crossed Aramingo Avenue and went into the eastern plant of the company.

Uriah Smith Stephens and the Founding of the Knights of Labor

The Noble Order of the Knights of Labor was the largest and one of the most important labor movements in America in the nineteenth century. Founded in 1869, in Kensington near Coral and Sergeant Streets, by 1885, its membership had reached over three-quarters of a million workers. Its founder was a local resident by the name of Uriah Smith Stephens.

Stephens was born on August 3, 1821, in Cape May County, New Jersey. His parents were Baptists, and it was their intention to have Uriah train for the ministry, of which his education was started on for this purpose. With the financial collapse of the American economy during the Panic of 1837, his

Portrait of Uriah Smith Stephens (1821–1882), who lived at 2551 Coral Street, just above Sergeant Street, at the time he founded the Knights of Labor.

parents suffered financial reverses, and Uriah had to be indentured out as an apprentice to learn a trade. In 1845, he relocated to Philadelphia, where he resided for most of the rest of his life.

In 1864, Stephens became involved with the Masons and eventually became a Sublime Degree of Master Mason in the Kensington Lodge No. 211. His background and knowledge of Masonry would be used by him when he set out to found the Knights of Labor.

At the last meeting of the Garment-Cutters' Union in 1869 (of which Stephens was a member), and after a motion to disband had prevailed, Stephens invited a few members who were present to meet with him in order to discuss his plan of a new organization. This meeting was held at Stephens's home at 2347 Coral Street on the evening of November 25, 1869. The address numbering system changed in the later nineteenth century, and this

The 2551 Coral Street home (at center), where, on November 25, 1869, Thanksgiving evening, Uriah Smith Stephens founded the Knights of Labor.

2347 Coral Street address would be today's 2551 Coral Street, the eighth house north of Sergeant Street on the east side of Coral.

At this founding meeting, Stephens laid before his guests his plan of a new organization, the Noble and Holy Order of the Knights of Labor. It was a new departure in labor organization, founded on the principle of local assembly. He described what he considered to be a tendency toward large combinations of "capital" and argued that the trades-union form of organization was like "a bundle of sticks when unbound—weak and powerless to resist" the large combination put together by business. The remedies he advocated must "come largely through legislation and a process of education on the part of wage-workers first, to fit them properly for the work of organization." To this end, he urged "the creation of Local Assembly as the primary school of labor."

Stephens's associates, who agreed to form a secret society to take the place of the disbanded Garment-cutters' Union, were James L. Wright, Robert C. Macauley, Joseph S. Kennedy, William Cook, Robert W. Keen and James M. Hilsee. Stephens brought into the Knights of Labor the rituals of Masonry, especially the secrecy in the forms of ceremonies that were observed.

The first local assembly was founded in 1873 among the original associates, all garment-cutters, with the addition of several painters, plumbers and paperhangers. After one year, the membership grew to sixty-nine. The second local assembly was organized by ship carpenters and caulkers at the local Cramp Shipyard. Twenty assemblies were founded in 1873, made up individually of various trades.

Previous to 1875, 52 locals were organized in Philadelphia and about 250 in other parts of the country, principally in the mining regions of Pennsylvania, West Virginia, Indiana and Illinois. At this point, the locals were organized into districts, and then a general assembly was founded and national conventions were begun. At the first convention, Stephens was elected grand master workman.

Around this time there was conflict with the Catholic Church. In order to make the organization appeal better to Catholics and to gain support of the Catholic Church, all Biblical and scriptural rituals were removed. Stephens disagreed with these changes. He also disagreed with the idea to go public with the Order, so he resigned.

Stephens was replaced by Terence V. Powderly, who led the order to new heights. The order took on new strength, and by 1879, there were 23 district assemblies and about 1,300 local assemblies. About the year 1881, it went public and stopped working in secrecy. By 1885, it boasted 160 district assemblies, 9,000 local assemblies and over 750,000 members.

Uriah S. Stephens died on February 13, 1882, at his Coral Street home. He was buried at Mount Peace Cemetery. At the time of his death, he was estranged from the order he had founded and guided for nearly a decade. Nevertheless, he was still revered by many Knights. As a result, when the general assembly convened in Richmond, Virginia, in 1886, it voted to appropriate $10,000 to erect a home for the family of its founder.

Frederick W. Fritzsche and the Philadelphia Labor Lyceum

The riverward neighborhoods of the Northern Liberties and Kensington can boast of having some of the oldest labor temples in the city. A *Philadelphia Inquirer* article dated October 15, 1899, sheds light onto the early history of these labor temples, founded by German immigrants.

The German-organized workingmen of Philadelphia had three branches of their Labor Lyceum Association: the headquarters at Sixth and Brown Streets; the Kensington Labor Lyceum, at Second and Cambria Streets; and a rented quarters at Wharton Street and Passyunk Avenue for the Southwark Labor Lyceum.

Frederick W. Fritzsche, an exiled member of the German Reichstadt (House of Representatives), played a prominent part in the organization of the Labor Lyceum at Sixth and Brown Streets. Fritzsche was born in 1825 in Germany, and when he died in 1905, thousands of trade unionists marched through the streets of Philadelphia on a rainy day for his funeral.

Fritzsche was exiled by the German government for his socialist thinking and came to America, where he quickly became active in trade union activities in his adopted home of Philadelphia. "The United German Trades, the central organization of the Teutonic craftsmen, had been in existence about five years when the urgent need of a common hall for meeting purposes was felt." A meeting of various representatives of the involved unions was held at Fritzsche's house at 325 Callowhill Street in 1887 in order to determine a suitable building for their newly founded Labor Lyceum Association.

The Labor Lyceum was a laborers' club, a place where laborers gathered and organized against the manufacturers. In Kensington in particular, it was a place for the various textile unions of the mill district. The Kensington textile workers appeared to have been a special group within the city as a whole, probably due to the fact that there were so many of them. Some of the meetings at the Labor Lyceum attracted thousands.

After a couple of years of renting quarters, the Labor Lyceum Association found a new home in the old home of the congregation of the Reform Temple Keneseth Israel, at 809–817 North Sixth Street. The building was purchased in 1893, and the house adjoining, at 819 North Sixth Street, was also rented as an "administration building, and to provide quarters for the janitor." Besides a meeting hall, the building housed the lyceum's "valuable library of 1700 volumes," mostly in German. In addition, several of the individual unions had libraries of their own. Evening courses were offered in English and carried on during the winter months, as was a series of lectures and instructions in drawing.

The first floor contained seven meeting rooms for the unions. The assembly hall was on the second floor and, with the galleries, could seat 1,500 people. The hall was rented out during the winter months for balls, entertainments and other purposes, which provided a nice sum to the treasury of the Labor Lyceum. Membership in the Labor Lyceum was confined to "the trades' unionists occupying it," all of whom used it for a meeting place, except Textile Union, No. 8, which convened at its own headquarters at the Kensington Labor Lyceum at Second and Cambria Streets. Each union was assessed a tax for the support of the lyceum.

Connected with the lyceum was a German singing society, the Arbeiter Maennerchor, which was made up of the wives and daughters of the members. They maintained a Ladies' Labor Lyceum Association, which constituted a ladies' aid society, whose principal duty was to set up programming and various forms of entertainment that would provide funds for the lyceum.

Kensington's Labor Lyceum was housed at 2916 North Second Street and was erected about 1896. Five lots were purchased in May 1895, and bids for construction were put out in March 1896. We can assume that the lyceum was constructed soon after.

In 1898, it was reported that the Kensington Labor Lyceum Association was preparing for its annual pork lunch and peasant ball: "Their hog killing will be held at Second and Cambria streets, to be followed with all the business of sausage making after the manner of the peasants in the Fatherland. The costumes and scenes are to be represented at the ball."

Mother Jones spoke at the Kensington Labor Lyceum on June 15 and 16, 1903, during a heated textile strike. This annoyed some textile unions, which denounced the socialists, including Mother Jones, for turning the strike rally into a socialists' agenda. Kensington has had a long labor history filled with riotous labor strikes.

THE VIOLENT CRAMP SHIPYARD STRIKE OF 1920–1921

In what was described as a "dingy, barren hall of a political club" in Fishtown, 1,200 women met in February 1921 to organize a women's auxiliary association for their striking Cramp Shipyard worker husbands, fathers and sons. For the first time, these women had been offered a place in the industrial movement. It was described that they "sat spellbound by a new idea." This women's auxiliary movement followed a like movement in England.

Founded in 1830, Cramp Shipyard had been employing many neighborhood residents for several generations. However, by World War I, the yard had ceased to become a family affair and was out of the hands of the Cramp family. It had become a corporation where the bottom line meant more than the generational ties to the community.

Due to federal war contracts that Cramp had received during World War I, it was required to meet federal labor rules that allowed workers to organize. In the face of decreasing employment due to the drying up of government contracts after the war (1,500 workers had already been laid off) and the overall reduction of the size of the Allies' and losing countries' navies (as per the treaty that was signed at the end of the war), naval shipbuilding became almost all but abandoned. Cramp was preparing to move into building merchant liners.

When those war contracts dried up, Cramp management was not as keen on having to deal with labor representatives and tried to rid itself of organized labor. A general strike followed, supposedly for the sole purpose of establishing the right of collective bargaining.

The strike, initiated locally without national union approval, began when four thousand men walked out near the end of December 1920 and the beginning of January 1921. It became one of the largest and most violent strikes ever seen in Philadelphia. Seven thousand men eventually went out and battled in the streets with police officers and state troopers, whose numbers were said to be one thousand.

By the close of World War I, employers' organizations began to abandon the idea of dealing with labor on the basis of an "organized craft." "Open shop" and "American plan" advocates challenged the right of workers to organize. Workers began to see their struggle in terms of a social problem involving labor as a whole. Their struggle concerned not only them but also those dependent on their earnings; thus, the idea was born to incorporate the women's auxiliary movement that had been started up in England.

The women's auxiliary worked on practical things, such as trying to solicit the support of the neighborhood. The women were the ones who patronized the grocers and butchers, and they reminded them that they, the women, were their regular customers and that it was a good idea for them to "interest themselves in the grievances of their patrons and help them through the struggle."

Two commissary stores were set up in the neighborhood by the women's auxiliary. Weekly provisions were rationed according to a system that was devised by the women. Drugs were also made available by a participating pharmacy, with the men who carried strike cards only needing to show them. The same was true for medical aid.

Another aspect that the women were helpful with was keeping the men on the picket line. As one striker explained, "It ain't no use talkin'…It's the women that keeps up our picket line. When any fellow gets lazy and his wife's in the auxiliary she makes life so miserable for him he just can't stand it. He has to get out on the picket line…And if she's afraid he won't get there she just goes with him!"

The presence of these older, married women—many of them mothers or even grandmothers—on the picket line had an effect in lessening some of the violence that was so often initiated by the local police or hired security firms of corporations. While there was less violence on the actual picket line, the strike wound up becoming one of the most violent the city had ever seen. Because of the heavy police presence at Cramp Shipyard, striking workers prowled the neighborhood looking for replacement workers. Finding them plentiful at the trolley transfer points, they beat them and then had running battles throughout the neighborhood with smaller police patrols.

The neighborhoods of Kensington, Fishtown and Port Richmond went into a semistate of civil war. Port Richmond resident Bonnie Dooley's grandfather James J. Dooley (1892–1962) kept a journal that recounts the Cramp Shipyard Strike. He wrote these memories shortly after the closing of Cramp Shipyard in 1927. His journal contains a number of entries; the one listed below deals with the strike that took place at Cramp Shipyard starting in December 1920 and lasting through the summer of 1921. In the words of James T. Dooley, we get a peek at those times:

Cramp's strike was a long siege. We had a few scabs in Richmond, but let me tell you—for none remained when it was over—I don't know of a single solitary one.

The front of their houses was painted—windows broken—then boarded up—and everytime they attempted to go out, the crowds collected—no wonder they got out. A fellow up the street from where I now live, was a rigger—he stayed in, coming home on a Friday night—it was at about the start of the strike, they were a little brave, he had a few fire-waters in him and accompanied by his boss a Mr. Anderson and Harry his clerk. They are attacked—he pulls a gun and shoots one fellow thru the coat. Mr. Anderson is relieved of $80.00 and his wallet, which contained a pair of "Rosary beads" though he was a Protestant. I think they were a keepsake from somebody and thru channels he said afterwards he didn't mind the money so much—but he would like to get the beads back—I kind of knew the fellow that got him and I goes myself to procure beads but he had already got rid of everything but the money. His clerk Harry an old man around 60, had been knocked down, now I seen a husky Polish fellow about to crash him in—now knowing Harry to be a very nice old fellow, though I give a scab no excuses; I saved him. After they are all done up pretty—the patrol arrives and takes them away.

In Richmond if your great great grandfather scabbed it—it was cast up to you, when you died it was always brought up in no nice terms. The women were out hooting and hollering just like the men—and I don't know of one instance where anybody was ever told on, for there was crowds about when some of these things happened. The sad part of these affairs—when one in the family scabbed it—it automatically drew in all his family and relatives.

Certain crowds gathered at certain places—all armed. Every day they would follow or have someone else to follow a fellow who lived a distance.

As a general rule they would wait till pay night—they would know the roads or streets he would take—and at the right spot relieve him of his pay—plus a grand trimming. These scabs themselves carried guns, and where it looked like he'd come back—four or five would lay in a nice spot—having a retreat like Napoleon, always open—and all would let go at once—then beat it—they never published in the papers of any accidents, so they really never knew whether he was dead or wounded. They came from other towns, some of them professionals and there wasn't so much of a holler. Though some of the strikers had got bored.

To-day Cramps Shipyard is closed—these fellows that scabbed it—have their own time getting work, for in some instances they suffer thru it. If you were a man who employed a certain amount of men—and found out there was one among them—that the other men always worked against and caused a lot of dissension, for your own benefit, in the line of production, you'd think it best to get rid of him—this has happened.

Cramp Shipyard had become dependent on military contracts during World War I. After the war and the signing of a naval disarmament treaty, many of the world's navies began reducing the size of their fleets. Cramp's lucrative years for government contracts were over.

The military contracts were so lucrative for Cramp during the war years that it did not matter to management that it caved in on every one of the 122 recorded strikes at the shipyard between 1916 and 1920. Even though labor costs had risen by 178 percent, the stock dividend on the company rose just as greatly, to the point where it gave a 150 percent stock dividend even in 1920. However, with the drying up of government money, Cramp needed to rethink its business model.

The shipyard was now owned by Averell Harriman's American Ship and Commerce Corporation, the Cramp family having stepped aside. It had no choice but to go into the less lucrative merchant shipbuilding arena, which was somewhat glutted. The only way for Cramp to compete in this new market was to reduce labor costs.

Since the shipyard was no longer dependent on the government, it did not have to have a "closed shop." One stipulation of the government contracts had been that workers had a right to union representation. No government contracts meant that Cramp could rid itself of the unnecessary labor costs of union representation.

In 1920, Cramp was in a good position to bargain for an "open shop," where men could work without the need of union representation. It had already laid off about 1,500 workers due to the slowdown in work, and there was massive unemployment in the metal trades that produced plenty of workers to compete for the shipyard's needs.

The union contracts were due to expire at the end of 1920. When Cramp made the announcement that it would be an open shop come January 1921, it was met with an unauthorized wildcat strike of hundreds of men walking off the job on December 20, eleven days before the end of the contracts. Cramp immediately dismissed the union committeemen. The union's response was that more crafts joined the walk-off. Several thousand men were now on strike, with a great many of them living in the riverwards of Port Richmond, Kensington and Fishtown.

The strike was not preauthorized by the fifteen various national unions that covered the shipyard workers. The walk-off strike was a spontaneous move controlled by what was called a "central strike committee," composed of one worker from each of the trades involved. The rank and file took full control of the strike. This committee did not allow the officers and business agents of the various unions a vote in the committee's proceedings. While they did not endorse the strike, the national unions had no choice but to officially support them. They requested the Department of Labor's intervention as well as supplied money to the strikers.

While the Department of Labor sent conciliators to the shipyard in late January 1921, they almost immediately knew that the situation was hopeless. Cramp's president, Harry Mull, was determined to rid the shipyard of unions, and workers were determined to fight him. The next eight months proved the conciliators correct. It was not until the Machinists Union voted to go back to work in August that the strike finally came to an end, but in the interim, it was one of the most violent episodes in Philadelphia's history, a literal civil war in the riverward neighborhoods.

After the workers walked off the job in December 1920, Mull began hiring replacement workers. The *Philadelphia Inquirer* of January 17, 1921, ran an advertisement that the company was immediately looking for riveters, holders-on, heaters, tank testers, chippers and caulkers, linermen, shipfitters and helpers, layers off, joiners, woodworking machine hands, ship carpenters, mould loftsmen, crane operators, ship shed machine men, bending rollers, mangle rollers, furnace men and others. It advertised as an open shop and said that men should come "ready to work." The length of their job was dependent upon "ability and desire to work." Men were to apply to the "Employment Department at Richmond above Norris Street."

Thousands of strikers and their sympathizers assembled on the streets of Kensington, picketing the shipyard. When a large contingent of police was assigned to the shipyard to protect the replacement workers entering and leaving the yard, the strikers shifted their attention to the streetcar transfer points, at Front and Girard, Richmond and Allegheny or Broad and Girard, which were a distance from the shipyard and had less police presence. Here, they freely assaulted workers on their way home, unencumbered by the police.

Later in the evenings, the strikers' "entertaining parties" would visit the homes of the workers "to knock Hell out of every one they catch, daub their front doors, and break their windows." The whole riverwards area of the city (Fishtown, Kensington and Port Richmond) was involved in the battle,

Crowd of Cramp Shipyard workers huddled around the intersection of Norris and Claiborne Streets in Kensington. It is unclear what the occasion was. *Courtesy of Daniel Dailey.*

as the Cramp strike came on the heels of a very bloody and bitter textile workers' strike that had already caused division in the same neighborhoods.

An organized group known as the "Entertainment Committee" was responsible for the evening assaults on shipyard workers. The committee was disowned by the leader of the strikers, Charles F. Scott, who stated that it was the creation of the Communist Party in Philadelphia. However, the Communist leaders of the city denied any connection, and Philadelphia Police's Lieutenant Bausewein stated that union cards were found upon men arrested in some of the assaults by the Entertainment Committee.

A contemporary newspaper account of the day described a typical assault by the Entertainment Committee:

> *George McClay, a foreman at the shipyard, who lives at 2831 Gaul Street, is employed at night. On Thursday night his wife carried his lunch to the yard. On her return home she was escorted by a policeman. When they arrived near the McClay home a mob swooped upon them. The woman ran indoors, with the crowd pursuing. Inside were her three children, the oldest of them ten years of age. Fearing for the lives of her little ones, she held the door against the mob with all her strength, but was about to give way when the policeman returned with reinforcements and dispersed the crowd. In the attack, however, windows had been broken and the front of the house damaged.*
>
> *George Fuller, a reamer, whose home is at 2209 Muller, was at home when the attack was made upon his home. It is asserted that 500 persons were in the mob. The front windows were smashed, the sashes torn out and finally the attackers forced their way inside. In the rear of the house were Mrs. Fuller and her two children, one three years old and the other a baby of eight months. Mrs. Fuller was momentarily expecting that they all would be killed. Once inside the house, the mob started on the furniture, tearing the pictures from the walls, smashing chairs and tables and destroying everything they could get their hands on. Fuller finally managed to make his way to an upstairs room where he procured a revolver. Running downstairs and shooting at random, he managed to drive the mob to the doors. At that juncture, a force of seventy-five police arrived and for some minutes they and the rioters engaged in a battle in which the marauders used bricks and the police their clubs.*
>
> *When the fight had ended and the crowd had dispersed, the police did not have a prisoner. It was found that a small boy had been struck by a stray bullet.*

There was another instance when members of the Entertainment Committee entered the home of a shipyard worker and surrounded his aged, blind wife, telling her, "You can't see us to tell who we are, but if you don't get right on the telephone and tell your husband to come off the job we'll wreck the house." Another home, where the husband was at work, was paid a visit by one of the members of the Entertainment Committee. The wife answered the door, and the man handed her an undertaker's card. She stated there was no one in the house who had died. The man replied, "Better keep it, you'll need it soon." There were a number of other reports of helpless women and children being threatened by the strikers.

There is no telling just how many families were assaulted, as most people never reported the attacks out of fear of further retaliation, sort of like today's "no snitching" mentality. The newspapers did report the more serious attacks, particularly on the police, or where someone was killed or hospitalized.

On January 19, 1921, four hundred strikers attacked workers of Cramp Shipyard at Philadelphia Rapid Transit's (PRT) transfer point at Allegheny Avenue and Richmond Street. The mob was driven off by police, but not before two men were badly beaten and several others were injured. The strikers had gathered about PRT's transfer point, and when workers got off the cars to change to other trolleys, the strikers began to jeer, hoot and eventually attack the workers. The riot calls went out, and police arrived from as far away as stations at Paul and Ruan Streets in Frankford, Trenton Avenue and East Dauphin and Front and Westmoreland Streets in Kensington. Twenty patrolmen and twelve mounted policemen were then assigned to Cramp Shipyard. J.H. Mull was quoted as saying, "There was no strike as far as the company was concerned, since all those that went out on strike were fired and replaced."

The next day, striking workers attacked Sickler Entriken at Girard Avenue and Shackamaxon Street. Entriken, twenty, of 609 North Sixth Street, suffered a broken nose. One of the strikers, Philip Truede, forty-two, of East Seltzer Street, was arrested and charged with disorderly conduct. Other workers went to the aid of Entriken. A riot call was sent to the police at Montgomery Street and Girard Avenue, but when they arrived, the mob had dispersed. Two others were badly beaten with blackjacks. There were now seventy policemen and ten mounted officers assigned to the shipyard.

On January 22, a striker, William Sweeney, of 811 East Livingston Street, was stabbed by Rance Pinkey, a "negro picket," of Seventeenth and

Lombard Streets, after he had struck Pinkey because the latter refused to join the strikers. Sweeney was taken to St. Mary's Hospital. A large crowd of strikers chased Pinkey from Almond Street and Susquehanna Avenue, past the home of Policeman Donnelly. The policeman stopped the African American and blew his whistle for help. A number of policemen responded and dispersed the crowd.

The union officials announced that the entire workforce of the shipyard had joined the strike, but President Mull denied the report. A larger detail of police was dispatched to guard the plant.

On that same day, a shipyard worker was attacked by striking workers at Richmond and Orthodox Streets. However, Giamo Mattilo, twenty-six, of 341 East Rittenhouse Street, happened to be armed with a revolver. He shot one of the attackers, eighteen-year-old James McTague, of 2843 Almond Street. McTague wound up in Frankford Hospital with a bullet wound to his stomach, and Mattilo was arrested.

On February 3, 1921, a small plane was spotted flying over the Cramp Shipyard plant, dropping pamphlets on Fishtown, Kensington, Port Richmond and lower Frankford. The pamphlets were described by Superintendent of Police Mills to be of a radical nature, and they feared the Communists may have entered into the shipyard strike. The pamphlets advocated meeting "violence with violence" and adhering to the strikers' demands. However, the next day, Captain Victor Dallin, who flew the plane, told the police that he was hired by Charles Scott, a labor leader, to drop the pamphlets. He promised not to do it again.

On February 4, Grover Reeves, a ship worker, was attacked by striking shipyard workers. Reeves, forty-five, of 4912 Disston Street, was beaten at Tulip and Palmer Streets. He suffered a broken nose and other inflicted injuries. The mob dispersed before the police patrol arrived, and Reeves was taken to St. Mary's Hospital.

In order to help quell the violence of the strike, Superintendent Mills sent 8 lieutenants along with 655 policemen to the Kensington, Fishtown and Port Richmond areas. The lieutenants would command the strike force and try to stop the violence against the ship workers who refused to go out on strike or who were recently hired to replace the strikers. In addition, 65 newly graduated policemen were sent to the Belgrade and Clearfield Streets Station.

Most of the disturbances that took place in the mill and shipyard districts were not at first reported, although the police knew they were taking place.

As long as the workers in neighborhoods kept themselves free from outside agitators and settled their differences among themselves, the police decided not to interfere. However, it was now felt that "pernicious outside influences of a radical nature" had worked their way into the strike, resulting in riots and street fights, which led to the police involvement.

On February 16, George W. Miller, of 2957 Memphis Street, visited a boardinghouse occupied by Cramp shipyard workers. He threatened to blow up the house unless they went on strike. Dallas Reid and Anthony Dean, of 985 North Front Street, were then attacked by a mob, of which Miller was a member. During the ensuing melee, Miller was shot.

On February 25, 1921, four strikers at Cramp Shipyard followed home James Riddle, forty-two, of 325 North Second Street. As Riddle was entering his home, the men came in right behind him. Their leader drew a revolver on Riddle, while the other three pummeled him with their fists and blackjacks. They robbed Riddle of his $25.25 pay that he had just received. Riddle was taken to Roosevelt Hospital for treatment of a head wound and a broken nose.

Earlier in the day, as ship workers were leaving a trolley car at Broad Street and Girard Avenue, pickets were waiting for them. Words were exchanged. When the disturbance threatened to become a riot, Policeman Lindermann, who was directing traffic nearby, called for reserves. Before the arrival of his fellow officers, several shots were fired on both sides, and clubs and other "missiles" were hurled. An elderly woman, attempting to get out of the range of the revolvers, slipped and fell on a snowbank, and she at first was thought to have been shot. This precipitated additional blows between the battling factions. Once the police arrived, they were able to disperse the crowds. Five people were arrested and taken to the Eighth and Jefferson Streets Station. They were all brought before Magistrate Carson and charged with inciting a riot and disorderly conduct. Those arrested were George E. Whipple, Thirteenth and Girard; Edward Floor, East Norris Street; Albert Jones, Frankford Avenue above Orthodox; Harry Sparks, East Fletcher Street, near Kensington Avenue; and William Haley, of Palmer Street, near Frankford Avenue.

February ended with more violence. On the last day of the month, twelve homes of shipyard workers were partially wrecked by strikers and their sympathizers. No one was injured, but two men and a woman were arrested on charges of inciting a riot. More then five hundred men, women and boys surged through the streets in the vicinity of Cramp Shipyard, hurling bricks, milk bottles and other items through the windows of houses believed to be occupied by Cramp employees.

On March 2, 1921, Magistrate Renshaw threatened to bar Henry M. Stevenson, attorney for shipyard strikers, from proceedings at Central Station. Renshaw accused Stevenson of making statements in his arguments concerning the strikers' rights, which Stevenson knew they were not entitled to, thus encouraging strikers to continue the disorder.

For the first time since the labor troubles started, an assistant district attorney was present at Central Police Court to hear evidence of the police against strikers. Thirteen men and two women were arraigned. The principal charge against the prisoners was that they were members of "wrecking crews," men and women who marched around the neighborhoods, battered in doors and smashed windows of houses of nonstriking workers.

According to Captain Nicholas J. Kenny, who had been in charge of the strike territory for several weeks, a "committee scouts through the district and when it finds a house occupied by a shipworker who refuses to strike, the 'committee' plasters the front of the dwelling with 'warning' notices and after nightfall the 'wrecking crews' finish the job."

The cases of strikers Charles Staley, Emil Schudden and Frank Ketchum were disposed of in court that day (March 2). These men were fined $5 and costs each on a charge of disorderly conduct after the police had failed to prove charges of rioting against them. Frank Shaugnessy and William Egan, both of Gaul Street, were held on $1,500 bail each for court on riot charges. Joseph and Victoria Sulkoski, of East York Street, were also held for court on $300 bail each.

Also on March 2, four men were arrested for inciting a riot. The disturbances took place near the shipyard. Fifteen had been arraigned, but only four were charged. James Logan and Bernard Devlin were held on $2,500 bail each after police testified that they threw bricks at them while the officials were protecting men moving furniture from a house badly damaged by alleged strike sympathizers. Charles Summs was held on $1,500 bail after testimony had been given that he piled bricks on a doorstep that morning and waited for a gang of workers to walk by. Walter Wagner was held on $600 bail after witnesses testified that he annoyed shipyard workers on their way to the yards, threatening to kill them.

One of the reasons for the continuance of the increase in violence was due to a large hiring of new workers in February. On March 5, a crowd of men and boys attempted to interfere with Joseph Smiley when he was on his way to work. Smiley, of 2508 North Marshall Street, was attacked by the mob. He pulled out a revolver and fired it into the crowd, wounding James Golden, twenty-eight, of East Albert Street, a striking shipyard worker. Golden was taken to St. Mary's Hospital in serious condition. Smiley later stated to the police that the crowd threatened him with violence first. He stated that one member of the mob drew a revolver first and fired shots at him. Other weapons were then pulled, and further shots were fired at him. He then drew his weapon and shot into the crowd, the mob fled and Golden was left lying on the sidewalk. Smiley was arrested but later let go on $2,000 bail.

It was reported on March 13 in the *Philadelphia Inquirer* that two men were wounded and scores of children were endangered by flying bullets in a strike disorder at Van Horn and Hancock Streets the previous day. The shooting was said to have started when a crowd of strike sympathizers heckled Frank Gorman, twenty-five, of Lehigh Avenue near Almond Street, a worker at Cramp Shipyard. The wounded men were Michael Fagan, twenty-four, of 1124 East Palmer Street, and John Grossman, twenty-three, of 1126 North Hancock Street. They were admitted to St. Mary's Hospital, suffering from leg wounds. Gorman was arrested by the police of the Front and Master Streets station after the shooting. He was found in a house on Wildey Street near Front Street, where he had taken refuge after the shooting. At a hearing in the night court at the Central Station that night, he was held on $1,000 bail, pending investigation of the case. Crowds of children were playing in the street when the disorder started. Quick action by the police stopped the melee and saved the children from being harmed.

Three days after Gorman was attacked, George W. Miller, who had been shot in February and was getting out of the hospital, was arrested for his role in the riot at the boardinghouse. He was held on $2,500 bail and charged with rioting.

March 25 saw a strange shooting related to the strike. Charles Smith, forty, of 2038 Amber Street, was shot in the head as he was standing in front of his home. Smith was a furnace man at Cramp Shipyard, and when he returned home from work he took a short walk near his home. As he was about to ascend the steps to his home, there was a pistol shot from a dark corner across the street. Smith fell unconscious with a bullet in his forehead. Neighbors picked the man up, carried him into his home and notified the police at Trenton and Dauphin Streets Station. Several policemen hurried to the home but were refused admittance by members of the family, who refused to make a statement to them. It was believed that Smith was shot by a striker and the family did not want to talk to the police for fear of further assaults.

Near the end of March 1921, the strikers began a new tactic. From then on, they would begin to accuse the police of brutality against them and, in particular, against the women who supported them. On March 25, four policemen were brought up on charges by the strikers. The police had surrounded Friendship Hall (Norris and Sepviva Streets) and broken up a peaceful meeting of ex-servicemen holding a strike protest meeting. Police Captain Jolly stated that he went to the hall after he learned that a meeting of strikers was in progress where plans were being made to create riots. The strikers said that this was untrue and that the police roughly handled one of the women in the group. Due to this, Mary Byrne of Frankford and Norris filed charges against Lieutenant Leonard McGarvey, who was promptly arrested.

McGarvey stated that he arrested Byrne for using abusive language against a ship worker. A person by the name of Emory B. Bartfiled charged Captain Andrew Jolly with conspiracy, due to the fifteen officers who broke up a peaceful assembly of strikers.

Hugh McBride of 2734 Huntingdon Street filed charges against Officers David Kline and Joseph Geiger for entering his store and, without provocation, beating him with riot sticks. The police officers stated that they were dispersing a mob of strikers outside his store when McBride called them "hard names" and afterward interfered with them in various ways, attempting to strike Geiger with a milk bottle.

The general thoughts of the police were that radicals in the strike were making up the charges against the officers as a way of trying to intimidate the police.

Two members of the "wrecking crews" were arrested on March 26. Christopher McGovern of Harold and Belgrade Streets and Albert Hinkle of Agate and Richmond Streets were held on $100 bail each by Magistrate Renshaw. They were accused of throwing bricks through the windows of homes of ship workers. A couple of days before McGovern and Hinkle were arrested, Thomas Crawford, of 2350 East Albert Street, was stopped by a gang who threatened him unless he left his job at Cramp and went on strike.

He refused their call, and the following day his home was attacked. Following a riot call, Policemen Deitelbaum and Smith of Trenton and Dauphin Station arrived to find a crowd throwing "missiles" through windows of Crawford's home. McGovern and Hinkle were arrested.

On April 7, 1921, a trolley loaded with shipyard workers was attacked by striking workers and their sympathizers. The mob—about three thousand in number, including several hundred women, some with babies—was parading down Girard Avenue. As the parade encountered the trolley car filled with strikebreakers, a number of the parade participants broke rank and headed toward the trolley. At that point, the trolley car was attacked at the intersection of Girard Avenue and Palmer Street. Sticks and stones were hurled through the windows of the trolley by angry men and women.

More then two hundred policemen, mounted on horseback and motorcycles, were called out to quell the disturbance. They encountered difficulty in using their riot sticks due to the presence of the women and the babies.

After the mob had driven the last of the ship workers from the wrecked trolley car, the marchers proceeded east on Girard Avenue until they reached the gates of the Cramp plant at Beach and Ball Streets, where they hurled stones at departing workers. The riot continued until extra police reserves dispersed the crowd. Clubs were used freely then by the policemen, with one man injured and six persons arrested. The injured man was John Kane, a ship worker living at 3900 Tilton Street. Kane was cut about the face and head and was treated at St. Mary's Hospital.

Two days later, on April 9, 23 men were arrested. The men were leading a mob of about 150 men and women and were marching toward Cramp Shipyard. They were charged with inciting a riot. The police dispersed the crowd with not much trouble and with no injuries. The police had been tipped off that the strikers were planning to attack the workers that day when they got off the job.

Even though the men at Cramp had been on strike since late December 1920, the strike did not appear to hurt the shipyard. Cramp officials made an announcement on April 18, 1921, that they had in their employ 5,400 workers, all they needed for the contracts that they had on hand. Harry Mull added insult to injury when he stated that the strikers were not Cramp's longtime employees but, rather, mostly men who drifted toward the shipyard for work during the late war (World War I) as a way to avoid getting drafted.

May 1921 was a relatively quiet month for the strike, with few incidents reported. However, on June 10, a crowd of strike sympathizers surrounded a motorcar containing ship workers, whom they threatened at Aramingo Avenue and Clearfield Street. A detail of police was forced to charge the crowd before they could break up the disturbance. Three men and a woman were placed under arrest before order was restored. The police then escorted the ship workers to the shipyard without further trouble.

During the disturbance, Mrs. Alice Dougherty, of 3126 Cedar Street, had her shirtwaist torn from her back by the rough handling she claimed she received at the hands of the police. The policeman who took her into custody (Officer Keenan) denied handling her roughly and asserted that Mrs. Dougherty had incited the crowd by catcalling and shouting names at the ship workers.

Morris Coffee, twenty-three, of Twenty-fourth Street and Indiana Avenue, assisted Mrs. Dougherty in stirring up the crowd, the police alleged, and he was arrested. Stanley Nedziek, twenty-four, of 3243 Aramingo Avenue, was arrested and charged with interfering with the arrests of Mrs. Dougherty and Coffee. Magistrate Renshaw held the three on $500 bail to keep the peace. Lawrence Sullivan, twenty-five, of Twenty-sixth Street and Allegheny Avenue, the fourth prisoner, was discharged, with the police failing to prove a charge of disorderly conduct against him.

Also in June, the icemen, milkmen, grocers and other dealers in necessities—who had been making living conditions hard for the families of strikebreakers at Cramp by refusing to sell to the replacement workers' families—were ordered by the police to stop the practice or risk losing their business licenses. Neighborhood corner stores were big supporters of the strike, as many of their customers and family members were strikers. Wives and mothers of the replacement workers told the police that it was impossible for them to buy ice or milk for their children, except at a very long distance from the home.

Persifor Frazer, who was directing many of the matters growing out of the strike at the shipyard, said that he was "unwilling to discuss the plans of the company." In regard to the refusal of some dealers to sell food to the families of workers, he said "it is simply a part of the campaign of terrorism which has been conducted in parts of Kensington for many weeks." Another official of the Cramp Company said that "it would be practically impossible to think of any form of lawbreaking or deviltry that has not been resorted to in efforts to browbeat workers in the district. Cutting off the supply of milk to infants, is simply an illustration of the regular work of some of the law breakers in their efforts to intimidate the thousands of men wishing to work."

On June 28, it was reported in the *Philadelphia Inquirer* that a Cramp Shipyard boss was repeatedly beaten and stoned by striking ship workers while on his way to and from work. Barton Yergey, fifty-two, of 2838 Aramingo Avenue, a foreman at Cramp, had been a union man for twenty-eight years. However, he did not go out on strike this time and suffered repeatedly for his actions. The front of his home was disfigured with daubs of yellow paint, every window in his home was broken on several occasions and his backyard was filled with old cans and rubbish, destroying his grass plot and tearing up his hedges. The foreman also asserts that the strikers poisoned his pet spaniel and continued persecution of his wife, whom they hooted and jeered in the streets and even in trolley cars, causing her to become so unnerved that she moved to the house of a relative, on the verge of a nervous breakdown.

After six months of this kind of treatment, in addition to receiving daily pelting with bricks, stones, overripe fruit and decayed vegetables, Yergey decided to sell his home and move from the locality. Several real estate dealers who put their "for sale" signs on his house were notified by strikers to "let the scab sell his own house." He finally found a buyer for his home, and he, his wife and their two adopted sons moved to a suburban town in New Jersey.

When the day came for Yergey to move his belongings, he was met by three policemen who were to accompany him to his new home. Word of the foreman's presence spread throughout the neighborhood, and within a short time, a crowd numbering one thousand persons had collected in the street in front of the house. Trouble started when a brick was thrown. The first brick went through the front window and hit Yergey in the back of the head as he was packing his goods. More bricks followed, and both Yergey and the policemen were struck several times. Yergey left the house, guarded by the three policemen, and attempted to make his way to the trolley. At Amber and Sergeant Streets, the crowd increased, and by the time police reinforcements had arrived, more than three thousand persons were surrounding the foreman and his small bodyguard.

Twelve policemen arrived in a patrol wagon from Belgrade and Clearfield Streets Station after a struggle with the crowd, in which the patrol wagon was used as a "tank," surging back and forth among the mass of struggling humanity. They finally reached the beleaguered bluecoats who were still valiantly battling in Yergey's defense.

At this point, a striker in the crowd appeared to assume leadership and urged the mob to take Yergey from the police. Policeman Mitchell, who was attached to the office of the superintendent of police in a clerical position and chanced to be with the raiding party, reached from the patrol wagon and nabbed the accused agitator by the coat collar. A fight followed, but the prisoner was finally landed in the station house. At a hearing the next day before Magistrate Renshaw in Central Station, the prisoner gave his name as Joseph Haines, twenty-five, of 2764 Martha Street. He was branded a ringleader of the disturbance by the police and Yergey. When arrested, Haines was without shoes, and his feet were covered only with a pair of purple socks. He was held on $1,500 bail. At this hearing, Yergey exhibited scars on his head and face, where he had been repeatedly struck with bricks when he attempted to go to work at the shipyard. A livid red scar from a burn received in the latest disturbance showed upon the man's neck and breast, where one of the rioters had thrown a lighted cigar down the back of his shirt. Yergey refused to give his present address, as he declared that his wife, who was seriously ill, would grow worse if the tormentors followed him.

July 2 found John Barry, of Dauphin and Belgrade Streets, arrested for assaulting a ship worker. Barry was held on $550 bail. Barry accosted Joseph McVary, twenty-three, of 1728 North Third Street on his way to work. Following an altercation, Barry knocked McVary to the ground. Policeman Schneider captured Barry after a struggle.

As violent as the strike had become, the ending of it went off with hardly a sound. On July 28, 1921, it was reported in the *Philadelphia Inquirer* that the Boilermakers and Iron Ship Builders' Union would no longer pay benefits to the strikers after August 14. This was the union that originally called for the strike. The *Inquirer* stated that this announcement had "completely collapsed" the strike. Soon after, the Machinist Union voted to go back to work, and the strike was over.

The economy had a lot to do with the workers going back to work. The shipbuilding industry at this time was not flourishing, and Cramp Shipyard was actually starting to lay off workers whom it had hired during the strike. Cramp Shipyard would never fully recover from this strike or from the ending of the government naval contracts.

Aerial architectural perspective of Cramp Shipyard during World War II, when the yard reopened for several years for the war effort. *Courtesy of Torben Jenk.*

By 1927, the almost century-old history of Cramp Shipyard came to an end as the yard closed. There would be a brief reprieve: the shipyard reopened to help with the war effort during World War II (1940–45), but after the war the yard closed for good. After sixty-five years, the sixty-acre site of the shipyard still sits abandoned, Mother Nature overtaking it, slowing erasing the memory of one of America's great enterprises and the history of the violent strike of 1920–21.

CHAPTER 3

Crime, Politics and Social Disorder

THE GREAT KENSINGTON BANK ROBBERY OF 1871

On February 2, 1871, thieves disguised as policemen stole over $120,000 in cash and bonds from the Kensington National Bank. The value of $120,000 in 1871 dollars would be at least $2 million today. It was at the time the most successful burglary ever perpetrated in Philadelphia's history.

The Kensington National Bank was located in a two-and-a-half-story brick building on the east side of Beach Street, a few doors south of Laurel Street. The bank received its charter in 1826. It would later move to the southeast corner of Frankford and Girard Avenues, where the Frank Furness–designed building still stands, occupied by Wachovia Bank.

The robbery began rather innocently. At the close of the day, a man dressed as a policeman entered the bank on Beach Street and requested to see the cashier, William McConnell. The police officer told McConnell to keep a watch out, as there were suspicious characters in the neighborhood. The policeman left, and McConnell told his watchmen to be cautious as there might be a burglary planned for that night.

At seven o'clock that evening, two men—the policeman who had visited the bank earlier in the day and another man, also dressed as a police officer—knocked on the bank's door. Morris Murphy, one of the watchmen, answered the door, and the men asked to see John Holmes. Holmes was the other watchman on duty. He had spoken earlier in the day to the police

The Kensington National Bank (chartered in 1826) at its original location on Beach Street, several doors south of Laurel Street. *Courtesy of Torben Jenk.*

Kensington National Bank building, corner of Frankford and Girard Avenues, designed by noted architect Frank Furness. This was the second location for the bank.

officer about the suspicious activity in the area. Murphy, who was not at work yet when the police officer visited earlier, summoned Holmes, who recognized the policeman. Murphy let the officers into the bank.

After talking briefly with the watchmen about suspicious activity in the area, one of the men asked for a drink of water. Holmes went to the rear of the building to get the water, with the man following him. The other man told Murphy to go outside to see if there was any suspicious activity. Murphy did so, and while he was gone but a minute, the two men bound and gagged watchman Holmes. When Murphy returned to tell the policemen he had seen nothing suspicious, the two men knocked him down and bound and gagged him. With Holmes lying on the floor next to Murphy, both bound and gagged, the burglars went to work.

A third man appeared at the door of the bank with burglar's tools, and the men went to work prying the doors off uninsured safety deposit boxes. They picked out only the cash and bonds that were easily negotiable and jewelry. From half past seven in the evening until three o'clock in the morning, the three burglars worked hard at trying to break open the main safe where the bank stored about $1 million in cash ($18 million in today's money). The men were not able to bust it open and were forced to leave with only $120,000 in cash, bonds and valuables.

The noise that the men made in opening the safe went unnoticed, as Murphy the watchman was a shoemaker by day and was in the habit of working in the bank at night. Neighbors, upon hearing the noise coming from the bank, assumed it to be Murphy working at his shoemaker's table.

Both of the watchmen were over sixty years old. The bank suspended Murphy for allowing the thieves to enter after hours but did not punish Holmes. Murphy had worked for the bank for seven years and felt he was treated unfairly by the suspension as, after all, the other watchman said that he knew the men and that is why he let them in. Also, Murphy felt that cashier McConnell earlier in the day should have reported to the local police precinct about the tip on suspicious activity in the area. If McConnell had reported to the lieutenant at the local police station, he would have found out that the police officers were frauds.

Murphy lost $600.00 of his own money, plus $500.00 he was holding in his safety box for a woman's beneficial society, plus $435.55 that belonged to the Wesleyan Burial Ground Association (one of the burial grounds at the old Hanover Street Burial Grounds, now Hetzell's Playground), plus his job.

Leads on the robbery were flat. The police were dumbfounded. They had never experienced a robbery where the thieves were disguised as policemen. Investigations turned inward, and they got a break when an actual policeman, Henry Monies, was arrested for a robbery in Norristown, Pennsylvania. Monies was arrested for public drunkenness a couple of years after the Kensington Bank robbery and found to have some property on his person that tied him to the Norristown robbery. While serving his eight-year sentence at the old Eastern State Penitentiary, Murphy and Holmes, the watchmen at the time of the Kensington robbery, visited Monies and identified him as one of the Kensington Bank robbers. Upon finishing his Norristown robbery charge in 1883, he was promptly arrested and convicted for the Kensington Bank robbery.

In searching for the other robber, information was obtained that the Blue Shirt Gang, a gang that was headquartered on Locust Street in Center City, had carried out the Kensington Bank robbery. The gang had two groups of their own thieves fighting among themselves trying to rob the Kensington Bank. The robbery ring had some homegrown talent but also consisted of a number of out-of-town professionals. The organization was led by George Adams, alias George Williams, alias "Brockie George."

Brockie George first appeared in Philadelphia in 1869, by way of New York, but the Blue Shirt Gang predated him. It had been organized since the outbreak of the Civil War (about 1861) and had scattered agents across the United States. Within the police departments in all the principal cities, gang members had those who gave them information and protection, and for this protection, 10 percent of every robbery was deducted before any division was made. Among the robbers, a second apportionment was made of 5 percent and was paid to a treasurer to be used for lawyers or bail when any one of the organization was arrested.

In July 1872, a store on Chestnut Street above Ninth was entered and robbed of $8,000 worth of goods. The police were instructed to search for the robbers. Brockie George was suspected, and the police picked him up at Tenth and Chestnut Streets. During a walk to the station, George broke loose. The police apparently never frisked the suspect, and a running gun battle ensued through the streets of Center City between Sixth and Eighth Streets and Sansom and Walnut Streets. Eight shots in all were discharged, but no one was hurt. George was finally arrested a week later, after another escape; he was put into Eastern Penitentiary. While in prison,

Brockie George confessed that he was a member of the Blue Shirt Gang that had robbed the Kensington National Bank. He died while serving time at Eastern State Penitentiary.

Another member of the Blue Shirt Gang was George L. Leslie, alias George H. Howard. Howard is said to have designed the Beneficial Bank robbery where the "swag" was a "round million." He was associated with almost every major bank robbery in New England and the Midwest during the late 1800s. Howard shared in the loot taken from the Kensington Bank robbery but did not participate in it. He was eventually murdered by two of his "pals" at Yonkers in May 1879.

Most of the Blue Shirt Gang was made up of men with Irish surnames. Two men by the name of Jim Brady and John Hobbs were thought to be the two other accomplices in the Kensington Bank robbery. Soon after the Kensington Bank robbery, the Blue Shirt Gang was broken up, with members forming their own gangs and continuing their lives of crime. Eventually, all of the former members went to jail or were killed.

The Kensington Bank robbery was a bold robbery, one where the robbers used disguises of policemen to carry it out. The robbery was kept in the collective memory of the city for at least several generations, often being talked about in the papers as "the most bold robbery" the city had ever seen.

The Brazen Rusk Twins and Their Destiny with Death

I have come across a lot of odd stories over the years, but the story of the Rusk twins is one of the strangest. It concerns twin brothers, William and Jacob Rusk, neighborhood toughs who grew up at 140 West Girard Avenue. The Rusk twins were born January 13, 1857, and on December 27, 1882, they committed suicide together.

William and Jacob Rusk were the sons of Peter Rusk, a shoemaker, who had lived at the 140 West Girard Avenue address since about 1840. Peter and his wife, Hanna, were the parents of at least ten children born between the years 1838 and 1866.

There were only a handful of families with the surname Rusk listed in Philadelphia between 1820 and 1860. All of these families lived in the vicinity of Girard Avenue, either slightly north or south on the cross streets between

Front and Third Streets. In all likelihood they were all related. These families would all appear to be German, as they were in a German neighborhood and working trades typical of Germans in those days (cobblers, butchers and tanners); some were also listed as Germans.

The twins' father died in the spring of 1877 at the age of seventy-two. It was soon after their father's death that the boys' criminal troubles began. Like with many twins, there was a very close attachment between the two young men. They were rarely seen apart and dressed the same. They both worked occasionally as shoemakers, the same occupation as their father. The only difference between them was that one had a slightly darker mustache than the other. On one occasion, when they were apart, Jacob became engaged in a fight on Front Street. William, who was several blocks away at the time, said to a friend that he felt something had happened to his brother and went in search of him, where he found him badly beaten.

The twins' "corner" where they would hang out with their friends was Leopard Street and Girard Avenue, which was just down the street from their home. When the twins came of age, they joined several clubs, both Democratic organizations. This was a time when Republicans ruled Philadelphia. One club that they joined was the Howard Club (Howard Street and Girard Avenue), and the other was reported to be the White Fawn Association, which from newspaper accounts appears to have been more of a street gang than a political club.

On February 15, 1879, the Rusk twins and their associates were attending an event at the American Mechanics Hall at Third and George Streets. A brawl broke out between a drunken Jacob Rusk and some other men. William and John Rusk (another brother) went to Jacob's aid. When the fight was broken up, William pulled a knife on a police officer who was trying to arrest him. William lunged at the officer. The officer dodged the knife, but Rusk accidentally stabbed and killed one of his friends, David McCool. William was arrested and tried for murder, as the commonwealth felt that since William had tried to slay the officer the murderous intent was present. However, on his deathbed McCool stated that he knew it was an accident. After a trial, William was cleared of the charges and released.

On Sunday, June 4, 1882, patrolman Joseph Jarvis came upon the Rusk twins and a friend beating up a couple of men at Leopard and Girard. Jarvis intervened and tried to arrest one of the White Fawn members. The Rusk twins came to the aid of their fellow White Fawn member. When the officer went for his gun, they hit him with a "heavy instrument," knocking the gun out of his hand. They took his revolver and then proceeded to stomp the officer severely while he was down on the ground. Officer Jarvis sustained multiple bruises and a broken wrist. He was never able to pin the attack on the Rusks but kept to himself the memory of this incident.

Eventually, Jarvis did arrest the other White Fawn member, a fellow by the name of John Fox. In the newspaper account of his arrest, it was stated that the White Fawn Association had its headquarters at Mascher Street and Girard Avenue. Fox was charged with aggravated assault and battery on Officer Jarvis.

Jarvis was new on beat in the Leopard and Girard area. He had started the new beat at about the end of 1881. He was an English immigrant and took his job seriously, and he tried to clear the local corners of the thugs who hung out on them. He gained the wrath of the White Fawns for these actions. Previously, in January 1882, after only a month or so in the neighborhood, Jarvis was stabbed in the chest by John Hughes, one of the White Fawns, for no apparent reason except for the fact that the officer was doing his job. He was incapacitated for several months. Hughes was arrested, tried and convicted. He served a three-year sentence at Eastern State Penitentiary.

The local newspapers stated that Jarvis had been assaulted several other times by the White Fawns. This period in Philadelphia history was also a time when Republicans ruled and controlled the patronage jobs, so it may have been simply Republicans and Democrats brawling in the streets.

The events that led to the tragic end for William and Jacob Rusk came on Monday, Christmas evening, in the year 1882. The twins were hanging on their gang's corner at Leopard and Girard with some of their friends. At about seven o'clock in the evening, Officer James Stirk was walking his beat. He asked the men to move on (the Rusk twins were now twenty-five years old). Most of the boys started to leave, but the Rusk brothers became insolent and refused. The officer attempted to arrest William, but Jacob came to his aid. A fight ensued. Officer Jarvis, on patrol nearby, saw the commotion and joined in the scuffle. During the fight, Officer Jarvis was stabbed and fell "with a groan." The Rusks and their friends ran off, with Officer Stinks firing two shots at them from his revolver, with no success.

Profusely bleeding, Officer Jarvis was moved to a house on Leopard Street. Still conscious, Jarvis insisted on being taken to his father's home at 1227 Cadwalader Street, as his wife was ill in bed at his own home at 1219, four doors down from his father. Dr. Lyons was called and examined and treated him. He had been stabbed in the left side of the stomach and a second stab wound was in the back, below the left shoulder blade. Dr. Lyons did not feel that Jarvis would recover, as both wounds were deep cuts.

The next day, Philadelphia newspapers reported that Officer Jarvis, thirty-five years old and the father of three children, would not recover from the stab wounds. A police bulletin that was put out on the twins stated that they were dressed nearly alike, in dark overcoats, dark pants and black stiff-crowned derby hats.

After the stabbing and assuming the police officer was going to die, the Rusk twins escaped to Trenton, New Jersey, where the in-laws (Mr. and Mrs. James Mills) of their brother John Rusk lived. Thinking that the officer was going to die and with their past crimes added to this new one, the twins thought they were surely going to be placed in a death sentence situation.

The Trenton police were given a dispatch on December 26 from Chief of Police Gavan that read as follows:

> *Arrest William Rusk, aged about twenty-eight years, five feet five inches, dark sandy mustache, downcast look, wore dark overcoat and round, stiff hat; also Jacob Rusk, twin brother, same height, both look and dress alike. Charge, cutting an officer who will die. Can be found secreted at one of your boat houses. They have friends in Trenton. Use every effort to get them.*

Having already pledged in their youths that they came into the world together and they would go out together, the twins decided to kill themselves. With the police closing in on them at Trenton, the Rusks hatched their suicide plan. They would tie themselves together and jump into the nearby Water Power canal.

Telling Mrs. Mills of the plan and where she could expect to find their bodies, William gave her some things he had in his pocket and then went outside to the yard and came back with about six feet of clothesline, which he told her he would use to tie himself and his brother up. The woman pleaded with them and tried to talk them out of it, but with no success. They bid her goodbye, and it was the last she saw of them. The brothers left the home, went to the canal, took off their hats and jackets and laid them on the ground. They then tied themselves up and together jumped into the canal and drowned.

It didn't take long for the police to find out what happened. On Wednesday morning, December 27, they were searching along the canal near the Water Power bridge and found two overcoats and two hats. At first the police thought the clothing belonged to some tramps, but then later in the day, Mrs. James Mills, whose husband kept a cigar store in Trenton, paid a visit to the police station with Mrs. Sallie Rusk, the brothers' sister. She told them what the twins had done. The canal was searched, and the bodies were found shortly after.

An examination was conducted at Trenton on the bodies, and it revealed a "cool and determined" manner in which the men drowned. "The feet were tied together with a piece of clothes line, and the wrists were securely bound with a silk handkerchief, which was accomplished by tying the ends together in a knot and twisting the hands together."

Two of the Rusk brothers took charge of the bodies. John and Charles came to Trenton and, upon seeing the bodies, wept like children, refusing to leave the morgue for a long time.

It was explained to the police and the people at the morgue that the fact that the Rusk twins were unusually bound up was a trick that they often practiced. They both were fairly good at the tricks of the contortionist. The bodies were said to have been in the canal for about sixteen hours.

The bodies were shipped back to Philadelphia, but not until several thousand curiosity seekers had viewed the bodies at Trenton's morgue

It was no surprise for the twins' mother. She had found out the day before that the boys had intended to kill themselves and believed that they would. The bodies of her sons arrived at Front and Palmer Streets' Kensington Depot in plain pine boxes. They were conveyed to the home at 140 West Girard Avenue, where a crowd of people gathered to try to get a view of the twins' bodies. Many lingered, peering in the windows of the family's home. Tacks of muslin were hung up to keep out the curiosity seekers, and eventually the crowd died away.

Inside the home was an extremely emotional scene, as family and friends gathered to view the bodies of the twins. Mrs. Rusk related how the "boys grew up together, remained with one another constantly during their school days, and had lived in close companionship up to the last, and shared death with each other."

The Rusk family tried to place the twins at Palmer Cemetery's receiving vault, but the trustees of the burial ground refused, stating that "the will of the founder of the place forbids the reception of the remains of persons dying by their own hand." Eventually, the boys' remains were received at the old Hanover Street Burial Ground vault, now Hetzell's Playground (Columbia Avenue and Thompson Street), but not before fully six thousand people had viewed their bodies at their home.

It was stated that it was the largest funeral ever in the neighborhood. Since it was New Year's Day, many people were off work and came to the funeral out of curiosity. The boys' family was long known in the community, and their number of friends and associates was very high, adding to the largeness of the event. The actual funeral took place at 2:30 p.m. on January 1, 1883, but the doors were thrown open for the crowd to pay their respects at 10:00 a.m. The throngs lined their way into the home and to a back room where the boys were laid out side by side in two polished walnut caskets with silver mountings. Because the room was small, the spectators needed to walk by the corpses in single file. They left the house through a back door that led to O'Neill Street. The twins were laid out in black broadcloth with black satin trimmings, white satin vests and ties.

The White Fawn Association presented two columns of flowers, two feet in height, topped off with a white dove with spread wings. All of the membership of the White Fawn Association and the Howard Club were present and acted as pallbearers and security.

All morning the crowds gathered until they blocked Girard Avenue. At least fifty to sixty police officers were needed to control the crowds. At 2:30 p.m., the lids were placed on the caskets. Six members of the White Fawn Association carried the body of William Rusk and six members of the Howard Club carried the body of William's brother Jacob.

Throngs of people followed the boys to their burial at Columbia Avenue and Thompson Street. The route of the procession proceeded down Girard Avenue to Frankford, then up Frankford to Hanover (Columbia) Street and then east on Hanover to the cemetery at Thompson Street. During the route, they passed the intersection of Girard and Leopard, where Officer Jarvis had been attacked.

The police tried to stop people from following the funeral parade, but the people took different routes, with large crowds at the cemetery in advance of the bodies. In an odd twist, many police officers had to stand guard within the cemetery to protect the privacy of the Rusk family's funeral ceremony, which took about an hour, from the throngs of curiosity seekers who had climbed on the tops of nearby buildings and fences to get a peek at the funeral for the men accused of possibly killing a police officer.

Oddly enough, Officer Jarvis survived his knife wounds; thus, the twins seem to have killed themselves for nothing. Newspapers reported that the wounds would have killed an average man, but Jarvis had a "powerful constitution." While the Rusk twins escaped justice by killing themselves, several days after the funeral the police did arrest three members of the White Fawns for the Christmas Day assault on Officer Jarvis. They were: Jacob Stockberger, twenty-seven, of Leopard Street, above Girard; James Hamilton, alias "White," living on Pearce Street above Master; and Emil Wilhelm, twenty-one, of 1516 North Front Street. Wilhelm was already in jail for assault on a man with a heavy wooden mallet.

FRAUD AND FAILURE AT THE SHACKAMAXON BANK AND THE FOUNDING OF THE NINTH NATIONAL

The two structures on the southwest corner of Front and Norris are the remnants of the Ninth National Bank (on the corner) and the Industrial Trust, Title and Savings Company (the building south of the bank). The Ninth Bank was founded by a group of Kensington textile manufacturers. It started its operations on August 1, 1885. The Industrial Trust, Title and Savings Company had a very similar board with many overlapping members of the Ninth Bank. It was founded soon after the Ninth Bank.

The new bank was meant to replace the old Shackamaxon Bank, which had been suspended in May 1885. This bank had originally been located on the east side of Frankford Avenue, just north of Palmer Street and next to the original buildings of St. Mary's Hospital.

The Shackamaxon Bank's suspension was due to its accounts being overdrawn by $200,000. The founder of the Shackamaxon Bank, William Bumm, a local politician from an old Kensington family, ran the bank as a private affair, keeping much of its internal workings to himself. When he died, the true nature of the bank's finances was revealed. The bank was holding $115,000 worth of notes from Bumm, as well as $88,000 worth of notes from a Joseph Conlin, a street-cleaning contractor, who did not even own a bank account.

A number of Kensington's textile manufacturers had deposits in the Shackamaxon Bank. When it failed, these manufacturers decided to start their own bank as a way to have easy access to loans, short or long term, when needed.

According to historian Philip Scranton in his book *Figured Tapestry: Productions, Markets, and Power in Philadelphia Textiles, 1885–1941,* the Ninth National Bank was formed almost entirely by textile capital in 1885. Scranton also states that three of the mill men who founded this bank were also board members of the "old dame" of banking, the Bank of North America. Ten of the Ninth Bank's thirteen directors were mill men, and they held one-third of the bank's capital stock. Textile families not represented on the board of directors controlled another 30 percent of the bank's capital stock.

The Gay brothers (Park Carpet Mills at Norris and Howard Streets), together with John Dickey and Charles Porter (Porter and Dickey, also at Norris and Howard), partners in a "cheviots and cottonades enterprise," were the largest investors, with each business holding over three hundred shares of a possible three thousand available. James Doak (Kensington Standard Worsted Mill, Trenton Avenue and Norris Street), as well as five other textile men who served on bank boards, supported the effort by purchasing five to ten shares of the new bank. The "steady dividends (6–8 percent through 1906, more thereafter) and ease of access to the loan committee, encouraged the leaders to continue their board roles" in the new bank. According to Scranton, "None of these men had visions of financial grandeur. They, like others of their colleagues, simply erected a modest bank to remedy their credit difficulties."

Scranton tells us, "Ownership of the bank was divided among 115 to 120 individuals for the first thirty years. With the death of most of the founders, ca. 1910–1920, and the expansion of stock to 5,000 shares in two steps after 1917, ownership was further dispersed to above 250 after 1920."

In 1923, the Ninth National Bank surrendered its national charter to merge with the Ninth Title and Trust Company as the Ninth Bank and Trust Company (the Trust building next to the bank), which appears to have lasted until at least 1953, when it was taken over by PNB (Philadelphia National Bank), which in turn was taken over by CoreStates in the mid-1980s.

Today the bank sits empty, its grandeur long gone. The building is decrepit and has been abandoned for many years.

THE A.C. HARMER CLUB, KENSINGTON'S FORGOTTEN POLITICAL HISTORY

Many longtime Fishtowners know of the old A.C. Harmer Club that was once located at 1130 Shackamaxon Street, just east of Girard Avenue. However, not many know of its history. The club originated during the presidential campaign of James A. Garfield in 1880 and took its name from a prominent Republican congressman, Alfred C. Harmer, one of the leaders of the then dominant Republican Party that ruled over Philadelphia during the city's greatest years (circa 1865–1950).

Alfred Crout Harmer was born on August 8, 1825, in Germantown and died March 6, 1900, in Philadelphia. He went into the wholesale business before the age of twenty and, in a few years, established himself at the head of a large shoe-manufacturing company.

Portrait of Alfred Crout Harmer (1825–1900) of Germantown, longtime United States congressman. The A.C. Harmer Club was named by John Virdin in his honor.

Harmer first served in public office at the young age of twenty-one, when he was elected as a director of the public schools in Germantown. A few years later, he was elected a member of the Common Councils for the Twenty-second Ward and served from 1856 to 1860.

In 1860, as a candidate of the People's Party (successor to the old Whig Party), he was elected recorder of deeds for the city of Philadelphia. In the summer of 1870, he received the nomination of the Republican Party for Congress for the Fifth Pennsylvania District and was elected a member of the Forty-third Congress, taking his seat in March 1871. In all, he was elected to Congress fourteen times and served twenty-seven years.

Harmer was a staunch supporter of veterans of the Civil War and their families. He was a man known to have worked in the backgrounds, in committee work, rather than giving elaborate speeches on the floor of the House. Some of the committees that he served on were Naval Affairs; District of Columbia; Foreign Affairs; Coinage, Weights and Measures; the Pacific Railroads; Indian Affairs; and the Committee on the Library. When Harmer died, he was the "Father of the House," the senior member of Congress.

The A.C. Harmer Club's name had its origins in John Virdin, who helped to organize the club and was a one-time president. Virdin had always been active in Republican politics in Fishtown's Eighteenth Ward, where he was born. Both his parents died before he was eleven years old, and he was compelled to make his own way. For four years after their death, he worked on a farm in New Jersey, attending school in the winter. He returned to Philadelphia and obtained employment at Cramp Shipyard. When he was twenty-one, he met Harmer, the congressman from his district. The congressman obtained a position for young Virdin at the Philadelphia Navy Yard as a spar maker. Years later, when Virdin helped to organize the Republican club in the Eighteenth Ward, he named it the A.C. Harmer Club in gratitude to the man who obtained him his first government position

The A.C. Harmer Club was originally located at 308 East Girard Avenue, and it was there in August 1880 that a massive rally in support of James A. Garfield for president was held. In November 1889, the club moved to its 1130 Shackamaxon Street location.

In 1900, the club renovated its Shackamaxon Street building, which included the erection of a two-story addition to the front building that measured 24.0 by 44.5 feet. The first floor was to be used for gymnasium purposes and the second floor for a meeting room. The club also had new plumbing installed and new papering, painting and furniture. In 1903, the club had plans and specifications prepared by architect Joseph M. Huston for a new hall addition to be built in the rear of the clubhouse. The drawings showed a two-story Pompeian brick- and stone-trimmed building, 40.3 by 126.7 feet. Cloak and recreation rooms were to be fitted up on the first floor, and an auditorium, with a stage and dressing rooms, was to be contained on the second floor.

Besides its involvement in politics, the club sponsored local baseball teams and vaudeville entertainment acts for the benefit of the residents of Kensington. Large crowds were attracted to these events. The club also hosted the Elks in 1907, when 2,500 guests feasted on two hundred pounds of "succulent turtle."

As the original generation of the founders of the club died off and Republicans lost power in Philadelphia, the club slowly faded away. Today, 1130 Shackamaxon Street is an empty lot, its history unknown to the passersby.

KENSINGTON'S SPEAKEASY WARS

Many people probably remember the old Blue Laws, some of which the legacy is still in effect. The Blue Laws refer to the banning of commercial activity on Sundays. Influenced by the Christian culture that America was built upon, the laws were put into effect almost immediately upon the founding of America. Historians say that the term Blue Laws comes from "bluenose, a prudish, moralistic person."

When we usually think of Blue Laws we tend to think of the sale of liquor, but Blue Laws referred to many different activities, such as working on Sundays or using public transportation. Over time, the Supreme Court has ruled some of these laws illegal, but for the most part the states have either banned the laws or kept them in effect up until today.

Under the mayorship (1887–91) of Kensingtonian Edwin H. Fitler, ex-mayor William A. Stokely (mayor from 1872 to 1881) was appointed the director of public safety, and it was under Stokely's directorship that the city was determined to uphold the Sunday Blue Laws. When Stokely came aboard in 1887, he was determined to make sure that the sale of liquor on Sunday would be stopped. During the years 1890 and 1891, an all-out war

DIRECTOR RONEY'S WAR ON SPEAK-EASIES.

Many More Raids Throughout the City Yesterday.

Proprietors Growing Careful Under Police Survellance.

Officials Declare That the War Will Not Be Confined Exclusively to Illicit Liquor Sellers, but Others Must Obey the Sunday Laws.

There were a great many drunken men in Philadelphia on Saturday night, an abnormal number, so experts said, but Director of Public Safety George Roney, who came up from Atlantic City yesterday morning to thoroughly investigate the movements of the police under his control, found only one drunken man at Fifth and Chestnut streets. He directed the nearest police officer to attend to the man, and he and his private secretary, James Hoyt, drove on to the Tenth District Station House, at Front and Master streets. Here Lieutenant Wolf reported that he had every suspected speak-easy in his district covered all night. One arrest only was made, that of Mary Kenau, who lives in the rear of 912 Beach street.

Headline with message that the city, under Edwin H. Fitler, a native Kensingtonian, had declared war on the illegal speakeasy. Philadelphia Inquirer, *August 21, 1891.*

was undertaken across the city on the illegal drinking places. The newspapers called it the "Speakeasy War."

Many speakeasies popped up all over the city. The term "speakeasy" is said to come from the patron's manner of "ordering alcohol without raising suspicion—a bartender would tell a patron to be quiet and speak easy."

In 1890, License Court Judge Willson accused the city police of not doing their job by reporting the activity of the speakeasies in their district. The accusations led to the police clamping down on the illegal establishments. A list of operations was forwarded to Director Stokely for investigation.

As might be expected, working-class neighborhoods featured greatly in the Speakeasy War. In Kensington's Seventeenth Ward, places like Hugh Boyle's at 1345 Cadwalader and his neighbor John Keenan at 1356 Cadwalader were on Stokely's list, as were Edward Boyle at 1535 American and James Gallagher at the northwest corner of Phillips and Master. John Haughey at 1348 North Second and John Smith at the northeast corner of Howard and Master also found themselves in trouble.

In Fishtown's Eighteenth Ward, there were found to be a number of speakeasies along the waterfront. On Beach Street there was H.T. Roberts at 1409, William Flick at 1607 and James Connors at 1615. Also, a woman found herself caught up in the Speakeasy War when Mrs. Wood, at the southwest corner of Palmer and Beach, had her name put on Stokely's list.

A block in from Beach, along Richmond Street, speakeasies were found being run by Timothy Sullivan and Dennis McIntyre—both listed at different establishments on Richmond above Berks. Also named were James and John Dolphin at 2556 Richmond and William Watson at 544 Richmond.

Elsewhere in the neighborhood, Francis H. Myers at 1115 Frankford, Mr. Mullin at 1043 North Delaware Avenue, Henry Belden at 458 East Girard Avenue, David W. Levy at 1453 Hanover (today's Columbia Avenue), Moritz Hoers at the southeast corner of Ash and Thompson and John Kill Cullen at 2725 East Cumberland were all caught up in the Speakeasy War.

Kensington's Nineteenth Ward, a large area running from Oxford north to Lehigh and from Germantown Avenue east to the borders of the Eighteenth and Thirty-first Wards, was found to have forty speakeasies, run mostly by Irish and Germans, including three women. The neighboring Thirty-first Ward of Kensington had half as many speakeasies as the Nineteenth (about twenty) but was represented by many private clubs: the Thames Athletic Club (Jasper and Hagert Streets), Turners' Club (Jasper and Ella Streets), Gladstone Club (Emerald and Hagert Streets), Mutual Club (Trenton Avenue and Letterly Street) and the June Club and July Club, both at York near Tulip Streets.

One entrepreneur came up with an idea to circumvent the Sunday Blue Laws. Selling buckets of beer out the side door was risky, and folks had already tried to buy buckets of beer on Saturday night, but they proved to be distasteful the next morning. This entrepreneur developed a three-quart keg, enough beer to hold over a family from Saturday to Monday. For those families where three quarts were not enough, he also had a six- or eight-quart keg, which he would deliver on Saturday nights.

While Stokely's Speakeasy War might have temporarily held up the Sunday Blue Laws, it's hard to imagine it lasted that long, particularly when Prohibition began in 1920 and started a whole new generation of speakeasies.

PORT RICHMOND'S BLOODY WILLIAM STREET

William Street in Port Richmond today is a small street running between Tulip Street and Frankford Avenue. Back in the 1870s, it was part of Port Richmond's Jewish settlement that centered on Tulip and Auburn Streets and came to be called "New Jerusalem" by Jews and "Jew Town" by non-Jews. William Street as it ran through this area was termed by historian Max Whiteman as being "the first exclusively Jewish street in Philadelphia."

A little east of "Jew Town," and geographically confusing things somewhat, is Cambria Street, which sits just above William Street. Cambria Street also used to be called William Street (between Cedar Street and the Delaware River). In 1906, this section of William Street was changed to Cambria Street. Cambria Street today stops at Melville Street, but in earlier years it went clear down to the wharves on the Delaware River, which, by judging from older maps, would have added several more blocks.

This section of William Street (Cambria today) between Richmond Street and the wharves on the river was a place that was known the world over by sailors. It was a legendary port stop, a place for sailors to drink, fight and womanize. It was also known throughout Philadelphia as a rather nasty place with some of the toughest street fighters in the city. While technically in Port Richmond, William Street practically borders Kensington and Fishtown, and thus the story is included in this book.

In an old *Public Ledger* newspaper article of 1902, the writer reported that Port Richmond's William Street from the 1850s to 1870s was "a pretty lively place." In the years just before and after the Civil War, there was "no busier thoroughfare" in Philadelphia. On most every Saturday night, William Street

The wharves of Port Richmond, a "forest of masts, and almost every hour ships arrived from or sailed to the four points of the compass."

was crowded with hundreds of sailors of every nation. All along the riverfront was a "forest of masts, and almost every hour ships arrived from or sailed to the four points of the compass." It is no wonder that the district of Richmond became known as the Philadelphia neighborhood of "Port Richmond."

Every other house on William Street was a saloon, where "fiery brands of whiskey were sold over the bar to the throngs of sailors who crowded the rooms, with their cheap adornments and smoky ceilings." William Street, Richmond Street, Bath Street and other local streets in the area gave Port Richmond a reputation that was almost international. In every port where "sea going ships dropped anchors the name of Philadelphia's most cosmopolitan section became a household word." Every nation on the face of the earth was represented in the crowds of "seafaring men who jostled each other on the streets at night."

The stores on Richmond and William Streets did a flourishing business, and many illicit distilleries also thrived in the neighborhood, with a good many folks making plenty of money in the trade. If the police tried to close one of the distillers, a near riot would generally break out, and it was not unusual to see U.S. Marines with drawn bayonets marching down Richmond Street to quell the disturbances.

Needless to say, the area of Richmond and William Streets was known for the "rough-and-ready fellows who stood around on the corners. Their fistic abilities became proverbial, and for a well-built man to say that he was from 'Bloody Richmond' was enough to strike terror into the hearts of the toughest kind of a gang in any other part of the city."

The United States Hotel sat on William Street near the river, and many a fierce fight took place in its barroom, including an occasional murder. Taking a look at several articles on the period, we find one newspaper article of May 18, 1871, telling the story about when William Foy went up to William Street resident Ebenezer Boyce and asked if he wanted to buy some fish. Boyce examined the fish and, not liking what he saw, "contemptuously" threw them in the street. An argument ensued, and Boyce stabbed the fishmonger to death. Five days later, William McCaffrey was knocked down, kicked and robbed while walking down William Street.

By the year 1900, William Street from Richmond to the river had changed. Many of the dwellings were merely framed skeletons, and the old United States Hotel was no longer around. The "swarthy sailors in great crowds" who sailed the tall ships were gone, replaced by the "big black coal steamers and barges."

Philadelphia and Reading Railway Company renovated its William Street pier in 1900. It was said to be the largest freight pier on seaboard, being 700 feet long and 170 feet wide. It could accommodate twelve thousand tons in storage for coal, merchandise or grain. This pier was only one part of the 140 acres of this company's operations in Port Richmond, the largest and best-equipped city freight station in the world.

CHAPTER 4

Medical, Health, Hygiene and Social Work

CHOLERA COMES TO KENSINGTON, 1848–1849

Recently, America was concerned with the spread of swine flu. Due to the possible dangers of such a disease, many are remembering the 1918 flu pandemic, known as the Spanish flu, which caused over fifty million people worldwide to die. Locally, just over 160 years ago (in 1848), Kensington prepared itself for a cholera outbreak or, as it is sometimes known, Asiatic cholera.

In its most severe forms, cholera is one of the most rapidly fatal illnesses known, and a healthy person's blood pressure may drop to abnormal levels within an hour of the onset of symptoms. Infected persons can die within three hours if medical treatment is not provided. Most commonly, the disease progresses from the first signs of diarrhea to shock in four to twelve hours, with possible death following in eighteen hours to several days, unless treatment is provided.

As word of the possible spread of cholera to Philadelphia came, the city government began plans to help prevent a violent outbreak. The Philadelphia Board of Health created a Sanitary Committee that was responsible for issuing reports on the disease. In a report prepared by the Sanitary Committee and published on October 10, 1849, the disease appeared on emigrant ships out of Havre in November 1847. By January, it was confirmed in the United States at Staten Island, New York, and New Orleans, Louisiana.

The Sanitary Committee also took measures to rid the city and county of possible nuisances where the bacteria could be harbored. The sanitary measures adopted by the board of health prior to and during the prevalence of the epidemic in Philadelphia, in the summer of 1849, were numerous. The report also sheds light on just what the physical landscape of Kensington and its adjacent districts looked like.

Preparation was taken in advance of the pestilence appearance, and nuisances began to be removed. Between October 1848 and October 1849, officials removed 676 nuisances from Kensington (and Fishtown) alone. These nuisances included: 257 privies cleaned, 10 houses closed, 33 houses cleaned, 61 yards cleaned, 76 cellars cleaned, 46 privies purified, 60 ponds filled or drained, 80 hog pens removed, 5 stables cleaned, 11 filthy lots cleaned, 2 filthy alleys cleaned, 5 manure heaps removed, 19 streets and gutters ordered cleaned and 11 slaughterhouses cleaned.

In comparison, the total nuisances for the Northern Liberties and Moyamensing were almost equal to Kensington, with 681 and 691, respectively. Spring Garden had the most nuisances removed of any district outside the city proper, with 1,455. The city proper, the most populated area, had the most, with 2,621.

Along with removing the nuisances that might harbor the disease, District Committees of the board of health were established. For the Northeast District of Kensington, Northern Liberties and Richmond, the chairman was Jeremiah E. Eldridge, of Germantown Road, above Fifth Street. Other committee members were Oliver Evans, William Street, between Point-no-Point (Richmond) Road and the Delaware River; Charles Delany, 43 Queen (Richmond) Street, Kensington; and William Goodwin, 305 North Second Street.

There were also druggists whose stores were selected as dispensaries during the prevalence of the disease. For Richmond, the druggist was C.S. Peale, at William and Richmond Streets. Kensington had several: George C. Bower, Third and Germantown Road; T.W. Vaughan, Queen (Richmond) and Hanover (Columbia) Streets; R. Etris, Frankford Road, opposite Commissioners' Hall (at Master Street); and E. Morris, on Germantown Road, Cohocksink. The district of Northern Liberties' druggists were John Horn, corner of Third and Brown; Benjamin H. Sleeper, Fifth opposite George Street; S.P. Shoemaker, Second above Noble Street; and George Snowden, corner of Fourth and Noble Street.

A temporary cholera hospital was also established for the eastern and western parts of Kensington. The hospital opened on July 14, 1849. Mortality rates for Kensington Hospital were 1–3:40, for Northern Liberties 1–2:13 and for Richmond 1 to 4.

By May 1849, two people with cholera were detected on a canalboat at Richmond, the first cases in Philadelphia. Kensington, with a population of 47,697 in 1849, had 218 cases of cholera, with 54 deaths. Richmond, with a small population of 5,529, had only had 39 cases, with 13 deaths. The Northern Liberties, with a population of 49,321, had 147 cases, with 38 deaths. In all, the city and county of Philadelphia had a population of 350,000 and had 1,418 cases of cholera, with a resulting 386 deaths.

In Richmond, the chief cause of the disease was its locality along the riverfront, its want of proper drainage and sewerage and also the character, habits and occupations of a large portion of its population, such as canal and river boatmen, coal heavers and laborers. In Kensington, the chief cause was the unpaved, ungraded and undrained condition of many of its streets.

THE CIVIL WAR AND THE FOUNDING OF THE HOSPITAL OF THE PROTESTANT EPISCOPAL CHURCH

Today, Kensington's Episcopal Hospital is owned by Temple University Health System, just one of a string of hospitals that it owns. At one time in its history, Episcopal was considered one of the more important hospitals in America. Today it's a fragment of its glory days.

The hospital was organized by Episcopalian Bishop Alonzo Potter, who, with a number of old Philadelphia families, saw a need for a new hospital in the emerging northern manufacturing districts of Frankford, Kensington and Port Richmond. The hospital's original name was the Hospital of the Protestant Episcopal Church in Philadelphia.

The charter for incorporation of the hospital was granted in 1851. Besides providing medical, surgical and nursing care to the poor at the hospital's facilities or patients' homes, the mission of the hospital was also to "train and instruct suitable persons in the duties of nursing and attending the sick." This would all be done under the instructions and guidance of the religious principles of the Protestant Episcopal Church.

Twenty-four of the original subscribers to the church's founding acted as managers until the first board of managers could be elected in 1852. Subscribers had been asked to donate at least $50 each, and the board was able to raise $50,000 to start a foundation for the hospital.

A large bequest came in 1852 in the form of an entire square block of real estate. The daughters of John Leamy, Esq., donated the roughly six-acre lot (and mansion house) where the hospital currently sits, between B and Front Streets, Lehigh Avenue and Huntingdon Street. While it was not intended, the old Leamy Mansion that sat on the property was used as the original hospital. The mansion house had been the home of John Leamy and acted as a summer resort for his children once they inherited it.

The Leamy Mansion was immediately put into proper order, and the hospital opened on December 11, 1852. There were eleven patients received during the first month of operation. It was a small start for a great hospital's beginning.

From a report published in 1854, covering the first full year of the hospital's operations, it is seen that in 1853 there were treated 180 patients, 78 of whom

Photograph from an 1869 book showing the Leamy Mansion, the first site of the Episcopal Hospital. The old mansion was demolished after the new hospital was built.

were surgical and 102 were medical cases. The average number of in-house patients was about 19. At this point in history, the area of Kensington where the hospital was located was still suburban. The mansion house hospital sat on a full square block of greenery, ideal for convalescing.

When the Third Annual Report for the hospital was issued in 1855, it was already felt by the managers that there was a great necessity to erect a new hospital. For the year 1854, there were 289 in-house patients seen, over 100 more than the previous year. There were also almost 1,000 "out-door" patients who were attended to by the physicians. The old Leamy Mansion house was simply too small to accommodate these growing numbers, and some patients were turned away.

Many of the in-house patients who were being seen at this time were poor Irish immigrants (169 of 289 in-house patients) who could not afford to pay for medical treatment. The patients were also heavily Protestant rather than Catholic (225 of 289).

The Fourth Annual Report of the hospital issued in 1856 shows that there were 313 in-house patients, a slight increase from the previous year. There would have been many more, but patients were still being turned away due to the lack of availability of beds. Again, there were calls made by the board for the building of a new facility. A building committee was formed, and monies began to be collected.

In 1857, when the Fifth Annual Report was issued, it mentioned that the start of the building of the new hospital had still not yet taken place due to an insufficient amount of monies to justify its building. The proceedings of that event were written up and published and include engravings of what the new hospital would look like, as well the floor plans for the main floor of the hospital.

The board of directors created a Building Committee made of up nine members. This committee met for four successive evenings in late 1859 and reviewed several plans of the new hospital. In the end, it selected Samuel Sloan (1815–1884) as the architect. Sloan was a leading architect and writer of architecture books in his day. One of his specialties was the architecture of churches and institutional buildings. On May 24, 1860, the laying of the cornerstone took place.

Sloan's plans called for a Norman-style building to be constructed on the western half of the property. It was to be modeled after the Parisian Hospital Lariboisiere, a celebrated European hospital. The style was to be "modified

to suit the purpose and character of the edifice," leaving out the "heaviness characteristic of the early stages" of the Norman style.

The original plan called for five parallel pavilions, but only three would be constructed at this time. The entire width of the facility would be 256 feet, with an equal depth of size. The first floor plans called for a central building where there would be a large multistory chapel, with chambers for the chaplain and an officers' dining room. There would also be an apothecary, library, parlor and steward's room. Coming off the center building there were to be covered corridors leading to two patients' wings that would each house thirty beds, a nurses' room, a scullery, a dining room and a library. Around the sides of the building were verandas where patients could convalesce. Each wing would be three stories in height, with similar accommodations on each floor. There were also extra rooms in the basement for special cases. In total, there would be about two hundred beds.

For now, the old Leamy Mansion would stay in place, acting as the hospital while the new buildings were constructed. The mansion house was situated halfway between Huntingdon Street and Lehigh Avenue, in the line of A Street (then called Filmore) if A Street continued through the property. A pond, oval shaped and one hundred feet in diameter on the long end, sat at the northeast corner of the property, near today's B Street and Lehigh Avenue. The rest of the grounds were their natural green. There were also several framed stable buildings and a boiler building that sat in the corner of the lot at Front and Huntingdon Streets.

By 1861, the foundation outlining the buildings was laid. The basement of the western wing was finished, and all the joists for the principal floors were in place. The brickwork on the corridors and first floor of the central nave were finished to the height of the joists. The chapel was nearly constructed to the roof. The eastern wing was likewise coming along but was not as advanced as the western wing. It was estimated that by the summer of 1862 the western wing would be ready for occupancy and that the chapel would be finished before that time.

With the outbreak of the American Civil War, the hospital's western wing was hurried into service. The government took over the completed portions of the new hospital. The old Leamy Mansion was forced to stay open to care for civilian patients.

In July 1862, the hospital started to receive its first casualties of the war. Of the first forty-seven soldiers received in July, all but one came on a stretcher.

Medical, Health, Hygiene and Social Work

A photograph showing the Episcopal Hospital's original chapel and southern part of west wing that was hurried into use by the outbreak of the Civil War.

These soldiers had been dangerously wounded near Richmond, Virginia, and were captured. Their wounds were dressed but once, and their meals had consisted of only flour and water.

Other trains began to arrive with wounded and dying soldiers. In August 1862, the hospital received 213 soldiers, 22 of whom died. In all, from July to December, the hospital treated 531 soldiers, many coming directly from the front lines of the Peninsula Campaign, still muddied and bloodied by battle when they arrived.

Of these 531 soldiers, 33 died, 12 deserted and 136 returned to battle. There were 103 soldiers whose cases were so bad that they were mustered out of service. Of the 33 dead, 7 died from chronic diarrhea, 6 from typhoid fever, 6 from gunshot wounds and 4 from explosions, where amputation of limbs failed to save them.

So began the first year of the new Episcopal Hospital.

THE PUBLIC BATH ASSOCIATION IN KENSINGTON

It's hard to imagine it today, but at one point, and not long ago, many of the working poor went to bathhouses to get bathed. Indoor plumbing was rare in the poorer sections of Philadelphia until at least World War I (1914), and it was estimated in the 1890s that only one in twenty houses had a bathroom with a shower or tub. Unlike other big cities, Philadelphia never had a municipal bathhouse system. What bathhouses Philadelphia had were managed by a charitable society concerned with sanitary conditions in the poorest "immigrant" neighborhoods of Philadelphia.

The Public Baths Association of Philadelphia (PBA) was founded in 1895 as a private charity group. PBA was founded in order to provide "inexpensive bathing and laundry facilities" to the "self-respecting poor" in the densely populated working-class neighborhoods of Philadelphia.

The PBA opened its first bathhouse in 1898 and its last in 1928. It would eventually open a total of six bathhouses in today's South Philadelphia, Center City and Kensington. By the year 1950, with most of the city's residents having access to indoor plumbing, the PBA closed its doors.

Sarah Dickson Lowrie, a wealthy Philadelphia social reformer keenly interested in "improv[ing] sanitary conditions of the working poor," founded the PBA. The PBA's first bathhouse was located at 410–412 Gaskill Street and was opened in April 1898. Gaskill Street is the small street just north of South Street. In 1895, this area was considered a ghetto, populated by recently arrived immigrants, many of whom were Jewish. The bathhouse was able to service nine hundred bathers a day.

The Gaskill Street facility had separate areas for men and women. The women bathed on the second floor, the men the first floor. Women had access to laundry facilities in the basement, but the men only had access to the laundry on weekends. For one nickel, you had use of a private shower for thirty minutes.

In 1902, a second bathhouse was opened and was located at 718 Wood Street. Soon after the opening of the second bathhouse, the success of these first two facilities encouraged the opening of a third bathhouse across the street from the first at 413–415 Gaskill Street. This facility was only for women.

In 1910, a fourth bathhouse was opened, this time in Kensington at 1203–1205 Germantown Avenue, just north of Girard Avenue. This facility was larger than the previous three. The cost was $7,000 for the building and $4,800 for the lot. Nearly four hundred individuals contributed to the building fund. Mostly Irish, German and English immigrants frequented this place.

After twelve years, a fifth bathhouse was built in 1922 in South Philadelphia's Italian section at Passyunk Avenue and Wharton Street. A sixth and final bathhouse was built by the PBA in 1928, again in Kensington, at 1808–1814 Hazzard Street, near Kensington Avenue. This Hazzard Street Bathhouse was the largest bathhouse built by the PBA and the most expensive at $108,798.

A 1931 PBA Annual Report shows that the Germantown Avenue Bathhouse had 70 shower baths for men and women and the Hazzard Street Bathhouse had 107. Hot and cold water with towel and soap cost only five cents. After 5:00 p.m. and on the weekends or holidays, the cost was ten cents, with extra towels at five cents each. There was no charge for children under ten with one of their parents.

The hours of the Kensington bathhouses were 8:00 a.m. to 8:00 p.m. Monday through Friday, 8:00 a.m. to 9:00 p.m. on Saturdays and 7:00 a.m. to 12:00 p.m. on Sundays. On holidays the hours were 8:00 a.m. to 11:00 a.m. During the winter months (November through February), the weekday hours were shortened to 7:00 p.m., with Saturday shortened to 8:00 p.m. and Sunday opening up one hour later at 8:00 a.m.

During the Depression, the PBA ran into financial troubles, and demands were higher. The association was unable to maintain its facilities. By the time World War II came along, many men went off to war, jobs began to be plentiful, incomes rose for working-class people, immigration rates were lower and indoor plumbing was becoming more common.

During World War II, the PBA sold off the Gaskill Street Bathhouses. In 1943, it closed the Hazzard Street Bathhouse and sold it three years later. In 1946, it also sold off the Wood Street Bathhouse.

After having further financial difficulties, the PBA surveyed the needs for bathhouses and determined there was no longer as great a need as there had been since 1895. The Germantown Avenue and Passyunk Avenue Bathhouses were sold off in April 1948. By October 1948, the Public Bath Association ceased its operations after fifty-three years of helping the working poor.

THE KENSINGTON TEMPERANCE SOCIETY

Throughout the early years of America, Americans generally drank wine, beer and cider on a daily basis. From just before the Revolution and continuing into the first several decades of the founding of the United States, American drinking habits changed. Americans began to drink more "ardent spirits" like rum, gin and whiskey. Distilled spirits consumption increased as the price for it dropped. Western farmers found it a cheap way to get their surplus grains to market. This rising consumption of hard liquor prompted temperance reform movements in the 1820s.

It has been estimated that between 1790 and 1830, the annual consumption of hard liquor rose from five to ten gallons annually per individual who drank. The founding of the American Temperance Society in 1826 is credited with reducing the rise of hard liquor consumption. By 1840, the annual consumption was back down to about five gallons per year, never rising above that level again.

Within three years of the founding of the American Temperance Society, there were about one thousand temperance societies throughout America, with close to 1 million individuals pledging not to drink. In the mid-1830s, Philadelphia had over thirty societies with as many as 4,500 members.

In 1830, Sylvester Graham, considered a "dynamic young lecturer," spent much of his time in the Northern Liberties and Kensington, pushing temperance reform. He, along with a Northern Liberties minister, the Reverend James Patterson, worked to reform Kensington.

Kensington's (Fishtown) involvement in the temperance movement started with John Vaughan (1786–1846), a Kensington shipbuilder and community leader. Like Jacob Tees, his contemporary in Kensington, John Vaughan began his shipyard during the boom in shipbuilding created by the Napoleonic Wars and the War of 1812. His original shipyard, at the foot of Shackamaxon Street, and his second yard at the foot of Palmer Street (later Cramp dry dock), saw their zenith during the years of steamboats and the first transatlantic packet ships.

Vaughan's shipyard was active from 1810 to 1846. Besides his excellent reputation as a naval architect, Vaughan was also very active in the Kensington community, helping to organize and serve as first president of the Kensington Temperance Society and acting as one of the founders of the Kensington Soup Society.

In the days of John Vaughan, the ship carpenters worked from sunrise to sunset, and it was always the practice of the shipbuilders to estimate one or two hogsheads of rum and one barrel of sugar in the building of a large vessel. This was without the provision that was always made for the vessel launching, which was a heavy expense. A hogshead was a large wooden cask and could usually hold between fifty-four and sixty-three gallons of rum. A barrel of sugar consisted of about five cubic feet. Merchants would regularly send hogsheads of "Jamaica or Barbadoes rum," which was ladled out to the workmen at about ten o'clock in the morning. The allowance was one pint of rum per workman.

In 1828, John Vaughan was instrumental in the founding of the Kensington Temperance Society of Philadelphia, the first in Kensington. This society was instituted on June 23, 1828, and by 1832 had eighty members. Vaughan was the society's first president.

Vaughan was a deeply religious man, a longtime trustee of the Kensington Methodist Episcopal "Old Brick" Church. He was always concerned for the welfare of his workmen. Being a man of temperance, he was able to almost entirely rid his workplace of the practice of drinking rum by offering higher wages to those who did not drink on the job.

A report about the Kensington Temperance Society, published in 1832, stated that there was one Kensington shipbuilder who was able to build eighteen vessels, measuring 3,300 tons, and repair many old vessels without rum, employing thirty-five men per day. This was undoubtedly John Vaughan, as he was the leading Kensington shipbuilder at this time.

Another Kensington shipbuilder at his time built eleven vessels measuring two thousand tons and did a large line of repair work on older vessels, employing on average forty men per day—without liquor. There were also two Kensington ship joiners who employed from ten to thirty men without liquor. The formation of the Kensington Temperance Society and the banning of rum from the workplace do not appear to have been detrimental to the production of Kensington shipbuilders and, in fact, were probably helpful for all concerned.

Besides the Kensington Temperance Society, Vaughan was also active in the Mechanics and Working Men's Temperance Society. That society was organized on March 17, 1835, and Vaughan served as a vice-president, along with fellow Kensington shipbuilder Jacob Keen.

SOCIAL WORK AND RECREATION IN KENSINGTON

Whenever we read about the history of Fishtown and Kensington we often come across the histories of some of the better-known long-standing institutions in the community. These institutions were started long before anyone living was around. A place like the Kensington Soup Society on Crease Street was established in 1844 to "distribute soup and bread to the deserving poor" and only closed in 2008. Penn Home, formally the Penn Asylum for Indigent Widows and Single Women, was established soon after the Kensington Soup Society and helped to make the transition to senior living a lot better for neighborhood residents. This institution is still open.

Another organization where this author once worked, and which is also still open, is the Lutheran Settlement House. It dates itself from over a century ago and still helps to support the neighborhood with programming for senior citizens, immigrants, women and working families.

Besides these three old-timers, there were many other social service organizations in the neighborhood in previous years. In a book titled *A Directory of the Charitable, Social Improvement, Educational and Religious Associations and Churches of Philadelphia*, which was prepared by the Civic Club, in the year 1903, there were over 750 pages of organizations that Philadelphians could turn to in times of need. In those times, before the rise of the welfare state and dependency on Uncle Sam, churches and private individuals took care of the needs of the poor.

Places like the Kensington Church of the Disciples of Christ—Elhanan Institute, the Kensington Day Nursery, the Kensington Hospital for Women—Dispensary & Training School for Nurses, the Kensington Women's and Girls' Socials, the Kensington Branch of the Women's Christian Association and the Kensington Branch of the YMCA were only a few of the many organizations that appeared for the good of our neighborhood.

The Kensington Church of the Disciples of Church (Front and Gurney Streets) ran the Elhanan Institute at A and Seltzer Streets. The school opened in 1896 and was a place for young working adults to get an education. It offered a number of elementary courses, as well as literature, musical instruments, sewing, office coursework and the sciences. Office work classes and academics were one dollar per month, with music courses five dollars per month. The school could accommodate six hundred pupils.

The Kensington Day Nursery was established in 1880 at 2121–2123 East Dauphin Street. It helped children under eight years old who had no support from their fathers. The fee was five cents, and it averaged twenty-two children at its facility.

The Kensington Hospital for Women was a place I wrote up in my first book, and besides its specialized practice of treating women's medicine, it also had a dispensary and a nursing school at its facility on Norris Square.

The Girls' Friendship Social, or Kensington Women's and Girls' Socials, was located at 152 West Lehigh. Its activities included Mothers' Meetings, physical culture and singing and cooking classes, as well as kitchen garden classes. There were also "social evenings."

The Kensington Branch of the Women's Christian Association of Philadelphia was at 2423 Frankford Avenue. It had evening classes in arithmetic, German, dressmaking, millinery and bookkeeping. The cost was one dollar for twelve lessons. A guild met "fortnightly for study and sociability." It also had a library of 369 books.

The biggest asset in the area was the Kensington Branch of the YMCA, which was established in 1885 and located at 1854–1858 Frankford Avenue, just below Norris Street, at the site of the former Bower Mansion. One of the main features was a branch of the free library located within it, housing the library and reading room, featuring eighteen thousand volumes of books.

The Kensington YMCA also had a game room, a gymnasium, a swimming pool, an athletic park and a roof garden, and in the summer months, trips were taken to the "summer outing place" at "Dwight Farms, on the Penn. R.R., 32 miles from Philadelphia," where you could camp and play sports.

The Kensington YMCA also offered a common school and commercial classes, as well as classes in German, art, mechanical drafting and textile designing. Its lyceum met twice a month with talks, debates, lectures and entertainment by its orchestra. As was usual in those days, the Kensington YMCA also had religious meetings and Bible classes.

The building appears to have been open daily from at least 9:00 a.m. to 10:00 p.m. In 1903, it had 849 members. The cost was five dollars for the year for adults and three dollars for kids under sixteen, but the kids had to be out of the building by 6:00 p.m. The memberships included baths as well.

Looking through this directory of charities and philanthropic institutions, it is hard to imagine how the work got done without the deep pockets of Uncle Sam, but it did. When there was a need, an individual, a church or an institution stepped forward and helped.

CHAPTER 5

Little-Known Kensington and Fishtown Celebrities

ALEXANDER ADAIRE, LUMBERMAN, ADVOCATE FOR NIGHT SCHOOL FOR WORKING MEN

In Fishtown, we have an elementary school at Thompson and Palmer Streets named Alexander Adaire. This school is named after a man who was responsible for advocating for a night school program so that working people would have the opportunity to go to school in the evening after they finished their work during the day.

Adaire knew how hard life could be on folks, as he struggled himself as a boy, his father having died when he was only a child. Alexander Adaire was born on May 7, 1834, in Philadelphia. He was the son of Irish immigrants Alexander and Ann Adaire. By profession, he was a carpenter and builder in early manhood, but for the last thirty years of his life he was established in the lumber business at Howard and Berks Streets and became the president of the Philadelphia Lumber Exchange.

The 1850 census shows Adaire as a sixteen-year-old boy living in Kensington's Fourth Ward. His mother was listed with real estate of $2,000, presumably property she inherited by the death of her husband. Alexander's sister Margaret was listed as twenty-two years of age and born in Pennsylvania, giving her a birth year of 1828. There is a record in the immigration indexes for an Alexander Adaire arriving at Philadelphia in 1825; this is most likely the father of our subject, as there are no others of this name in the city at this time.

Left: Alexander Adaire (1834–1904), Pennsylvania state legislator, member of the Philadelphia School Board and advocate for night school for working men.

Below: Alexander Adaire Lumber Yard, corner of Howard and Berks Streets. While his interest was in education, professionally he was president of the Philadelphia Lumber Exchange.

The Adaire household in 1860 included his mother Ann, sister Margaret and Alexander. Now at twenty-six years old, he was already listed as a house carpenter with real estate at $2,500 and personal estate of $125. He may have come into some wealth when he became of age, perhaps the property his mother had held back in 1850.

The 1870 census shows Adaire as a house carpenter and doing quite well, with real estate now at $7,000 and a personal estate of $5,000. He had purchased a home at 1414 Palmer Street, the same building that is today's Elm Tree Post. With Alexander in his household was his sister Margaret, his mother having died. Also enumerated with the couple was Sarah Mullica, the possible daughter of an old business partner.

Having worked his way up in Kensington society, Adaire represented Kensington in the Pennsylvania State Legislature for several terms and was appointed to the Philadelphia Board of Education in 1874 for Kensington. He served for twenty-nine years on the board, becoming chairman of the night school. Adaire was honored by the city by naming the local Kensington (Fishtown) elementary school at Thompson and Palmer Streets after him.

An 1913 image of the original Alexander Adaire School, Palmer and Thompson Streets, built on the site of the former Morris School, removed in 1892.

About the year 1878, Adaire married a woman by the name of Anna Soumeilan. She was a schoolteacher from the neighborhood who perhaps met her husband through his activities with the school board. Anna was born about 1844. She was the daughter of Elizabeth Quicksall Soumeilan (1821–1895), who was living with the Adaires at the time of the 1880 census on Palmer Street. Elizabeth Soumeilan was a widow by 1880. The 1880 census shows the Adaires' first child, Anna, having been born in March 1880.

By the time the 1900 census was taken, Adaire was still found enumerated at his old home at 1414 Palmer Street. He owned this home free of mortgage. With Adaire were his wife, Anna, and now two children, Anna and Alexander (born 1882). Both father and son worked together in the family's lumber business. The family also employed a twenty-one-year-old live-in Irish servant named Lizzie O'Neill to help Mrs. Adaire.

Alexander Adaire died on January 14, 1904, at his residence at 1227 West Lehigh Avenue. He spent his entire life in Kensington until his removal to Twelfth and Lehigh in the summer of 1903. His death certificate states the cause of death as "acute nephritis" with a contributing factor of "exhaustion, grief over loss of wife." He was interred on January 16, 1904, at Odd Fellows Cemetery Vault. The undertaker was the longtime Kensington firm of Titlow Brothers, of 341 Richmond Street.

Adaire was survived by his son Alexander Adaire III, who was a student at Princeton when his father died, and his daughter, Anna Adaire, who was studying at Bryn Mawr College at the time of her father's death. Adaire left his entire estate ($70,000) to his children.

During his lifetime, Alexander Adaire was a member of a number of organizations and societies, including the Board of Trade and the Lumbermen's Exchange, as well as fraternal clubs such as the Masonic Order, the Odd Fellows, Knights of Pythias, Order of Sparta, American Mechanics and United Workmen.

"The Rose of Tralee" and the Cruice Family of St. Anne's

One of the most famous of the nineteenth-century Irish ballads is a piece titled "The Rose of Tralee." The words of the song are often credited to C. (or E.) Mordaunt Spencer and the music to Charles William Glover.

However, for over a century, the Irish have told a different story, one that states that William Pembroke Mulchinock (1820–1864), of Tralee, County Kerry, wrote the ballad. Oddly enough, the ballad has a Port Richmond and St. Anne's connection.

The pale moon was rising above the green mountain,
The sun was declining beneath the blue sea,
When I strayed with my love to the pure crystal fountain,
That stands in the beautiful vale of Tralee.

She was lovely and fair as the rose of the summer,
Yet 'twas not her beauty alone that won me,
Oh no, 'twas the truth in her eyes ever dawning,
That made me love Mary, The Rose of Tralee.

The cool shades of evening their mantle were spreading,
And Mary all smiling was listening to me.
The moon through the valley her pale rays were shredding,
When I won the heart of the Rose of Tralee.

In the far fields of India mid war's dreadful thunder,
Her voice was a solace and comfort to me;
But the chill hand of death has now rent us asunder,
I'm lonesome tonight for the Rose of Tralee.

Mulchinock, who fancied himself a writer, was the son of a merchant family of Tralee. He fell in love with Mary O'Connor, his mother's maidservant. Her beauty is the "Rose" of the title of the ballad. Due to rigid class restrictions, Mary was unable to return Mulchinock's love for her, as his family would have forbidden their marriage. Mary also believed that Mulchinock would be ostracized from his family and their wealth if they married and he would come to regret marrying her.

Unable to marry Mary, Mulchinock became depressed. At a local political rally, a person was killed, and Mulchinock was told that he was wanted for the murder. He fled to India and did not return for six years. When he returned, he found that his Mary O'Connor had died from tuberculosis. In his despair, he composed his ballad, "The Rose of Tralee."

Friends helped Mulchinock out of his depression, and he married one of his old flames. He immigrated to America in 1849 with his wife and fathered several children. In America, he contributed to the *Literary American*, *Knickerbocker*, *Boston Weekly Museum* and *Model Court*, as well as local newspapers. He was also the literary editor of the *Irish Advocate*. In 1851, he published *Ballads and Songs of W.P.M.*

He could never quite forget his Mary O'Connor, and in 1855, he abandoned his wife and children, going back to Ireland, where he took to drink and died in 1864 at the age of forty-four. He told his friends to bury him next to his rose, Mary O'Connor, a request that they honored.

Mulchinock's ballad proved very popular, and in Ireland it is still celebrated with the Rose of Tralee Festival, an international competition celebrated by Irish communities around the world. The festival, held annually in late August, chooses a "Rose" of the festival, a woman who, like the ballad, is deemed to be "lovely and fair." The winning "Rose" becomes an ambassador of sorts for Ireland and travels around the globe.

The connection to St. Anne's is that Alice Mulchinock, the daughter of William Pembroke Mulchinock and his wife, stayed with her mother in America when her father went back to Ireland. She married Robert Blake Cruice, a Port Richmond physician. Robert was the son of James P. Cruice, Esq., of Lisroyan Lodge, County Roscommon, who immigrated to Port Richmond about the year 1850. James opened a grocery at Salmon and Lehigh Streets and died by 1859, but not before seeing his three sons, John J., Robert B. and William R., all become physicians.

The Cruice family were members of St. Anne's Church and had at least a thirty-year relationship with the parish. At first, John J. Cruice is found listed in 1856 with his brother Robert as a druggist and chemist on Salmon Street at Emory (Sergeant) Street. By 1861, Robert began to be listed as an "M.D.," with John running an apothecary at 74 Richmond Street. The third brother, William, soon joined the family apothecary as a druggist in 1861. It was this brother William who remained in the neighborhood the longest before moving to North Sixth Street.

In the summer of 1863, tragedy struck the Cruice family, with John dying from congestion of the brain. Many, including priests from St. Malachy's, St. Joachim's and St. Michael's and a visiting priest from Londonderry, attended his funeral ceremony at St. Anne's Church. John was buried at St. Anne's Cemetery. Over the years, a number of the

Cruice family were buried at St. Anne's, even after the family left the neighborhood.

After serving in the Civil War, Robert was appointed house surgeon at Philadelphia's St. Joseph's Hospital, a position that his brother John previously held, while also working at the apothecary. He married William Pembroke Mulchinock's daughter Alice in 1868. He and his family moved to North Seventeenth Street to live near St. Joseph's Hospital. Robert eventually became president of the medical staff at St. Joseph's.

Robert Cruice died in 1899, oddly enough while he was visiting a patient, General Pennypacker. At the time of his death, he was a Fellow of the College of Physicians, a member of the County Medical and the State Medical Societies and of Meade Post, a lodge of the Grand Army of the Republic.

Robert Cruice was survived by his wife, Alice. He was buried at Old Cathedral Cemetery. Several of his children who died young were buried at St. Anne's before the family established a burial plot at Old Cathedral.

LIEUTENANT COLONEL PETER A. MCALOON, ST. ANNE'S CIVIL WAR HERO

As seen in the preceding story, St. Anne's Cemetery is a rather interesting cemetery with some worthy inhabitants, as shown by the Cruice family of physicians and their connection to one of the most famous Irish ballads, "The Rose of Tralee." There is another worthy whom I would like to mention who calls St. Anne's Cemetery his resting place, someone whom I was first introduced to by Tom Prince: Lieutenant Colonel Peter A. McAloon, an Irish immigrant and bona fide Civil War hero.

McAloon enlisted in the Civil War on May 31, 1861, as a sergeant with Company K of the Twenty-seventh Regiment Pennsylvania Infantry. This regiment was organized on May 5, 1861, with a three-year voluntary commitment. The entire regiment was recruited in Philadelphia's Northern Liberties and Kensington neighborhoods, and at least half of its members were German. A number of both officers and men had seen service in this country and in Europe. One of the interesting things about McAloon is that he became a commanding officer of a largely German regiment, which was rather odd, as usually it was the Germans commanding Irish soldiers.

Tombstone of Lieutenant Colonel Peter A. McAloon (1839–1863), who died at the Battle of Missionary Ridge. His grave is located in St. Anne's Cemetery, Cedar Street and Lehigh Avenue.

The Twenty-seventh Regiment was attached to the First Brigade and saw some of the hardest fighting in the war, participating in campaigns that included battles at Cross Keys, Rappahannock River, Groveton and the Second Battle of Bull Run. McAloon also fought at the bloody Battle of Chancellorsville and served as a major at the Battle of Gettysburg. His military career also saw him at other battles and skirmishes, such as Hagerstown, Orchard Knob and Missionary Ridge, where he was mortally wounded with gunshots in his chest and wrist on November 25, 1863, while leading an attack on Tunnel Hill. He died on December 7.

Being involved in some of the worst fighting, the regiment was badly beaten up. Five officers and seventy-three enlisted men were either killed or died from their wounds. Another sixty-two men died from either disease or other causes. There were three officers and twenty-six enlisted men who were wounded, but not mortally, plus one officer and seventy-six enlisted men either captured or missing.

McAloon was a full lieutenant colonel at the time of his death, having enlisted as a sergeant initially in May 1861 and rising amazingly up the ranks in a short time. He was quickly promoted to full first lieutenant on June 17, 1861, and then to full captain a couple of months later on August 1. His rapid rise continued when he was promoted to full major on November 1, 1862, and finally to full lieutenant colonel on November 16, 1863. Three weeks later he was killed at Missionary Ridge, Tennessee, at the beginning of Sherman's March to the Sea.

McAloon was born in 1839 and emigrated from the town of Gorteen in the parish of Kinawley, County Fermanagh, on December 18, 1849, with his mother, Bridget McGovern McAloon, and his sisters Mary, Lizzie and Catherine. His father, James, had emigrated earlier. There would be at least two more daughters added to James and Bridget McAloon's family once they were in America.

The family settled in the Port Richmond section on Somerset Street near Amber and became members of St. Anne's parish. Having Peter die in the war took a terrible toll on the McAloon family, as he was the main support for his family. One family researcher stated that McAloon's father, James, had been a watchman for the railroad in Port Richmond and his feet were mangled or cut off in a railroad accident. Peter had been supporting his father, his mother Bridget and his five sisters, Mary, Elissa, Catherine, Bridget and Teresa.

After his death in Tennessee, Peter McAloon's body was brought back to Philadelphia, and he was waked from Independence Hall and then buried at St. Anne's Cemetery, where eventually his parents and sister Teresa were also buried. James McAloon died in 1883, and Bridget died in 1914 at the age of ninety-six. At the time of her death, she lived at 2026 East Somerset Street. Two of Bridget McAloon's grandsons became priests.

McAloon's funeral escort was the Sixty-ninth Pennsylvania Irish Volunteers. The regiment marched fully equipped for McAloon's funeral. They had been in Philadelphia on furlough but gave up their time to honor their comrade in arms and fellow Irishman. Prior to the war, McAloon had been involved in the Irish militia.

BILLY SHARSIG, EARLY BASEBALL
MAN OF KENSINGTON

Kensington can claim Billy Sharsig (1855–1902) as one of its own, as it was here that Sharsig lived when he first became involved in professional baseball. Sharsig was a co-owner, general manager and on-field manager of the old American Association's Philadelphia Athletics.

The American Association was a professional baseball league that lasted for a decade (1882–91). During its ten years of existence, it challenged the dominance of the National League. There was even an early version of the World Series that was dominated by the Nationals. The league was weakened when several of its teams left to join the National League (today's Pittsburgh, Cincinnati, Los Angeles and St. Louis teams). There was also the challenge of the Player's League, known as the "Brotherhood," the first baseball players' union.

Formed in 1890, the Player's League only lasted one season, but that was enough of a drain on talent and ticket revenue that the American Association folded. In 1890, the Athletics were forced to sell or release a number of their players, replacing them with "pick-up" players. They lost the last twenty-one games of their season and were suspended by the American Association, replaced by another Philadelphia team (Quakers) that had played in the Player's League. Sharsig was picked as the manager of the new Athletics. After 1891, the American Association folded altogether, and Sharsig went on to manage the Indianapolis team in the Western League in 1892 and in 1894, as well as several Pennsylvania teams in the late 1890s.

Back in 1880, Billy Sharsig helped to organize (with Horace Phillips) the American Association's Philadelphia Athletics. The Athletics played their first season at the Oakdale Grounds, at Twelfth and Huntingdon Streets, two blocks west of the old Kensington District border. For the rest of their existence they played at the Jefferson Grounds, at Twenty-sixth and Jefferson Streets.

Horace Phillips withdrew early to organize the Philadelphia League Alliance Club, so Sharsig, with Lew Simmons and Charley Mason (whom he previously knew), attended the meeting at Pittsburgh the year the American Association was formed. It was said by contemporary newspaper accounts that Sharsig played a major role in forming the American Association. While Horace Phillips gets the credit for inspiring the idea to organize a baseball club in Philadelphia, it was Sharsig who was able to get the financing to make it happen.

From the beginnings of the American Association, Sharsig became a prominent figure in baseball. Sharsig, Simmons and Mason became wealthy from baseball, clearing between $200,00 and $300,000 in just three years (over $6 million in today's money). It was said in 1884 that it was the greatest financial success ever scored in baseball.

William A. Sharsig was born about the year 1855, the son of William and Amelia Sharsig, Prussian immigrants. His father was a prosperous dyer and had ideas of putting his son in some productive business, but the young Sharsig became enthusiastic over baseball instead.

In 1860, the family was living in South Philadelphia's Fourth Ward, presumably not too long after arriving in America. By 1870, Sharsig's family had moved to Camden, New Jersey's North Ward. Around 1876, the Sharsig's family moved to Kensington, to 1718 Cadwalader Street, in the heart of Kensington's textile district, where both father and son worked as dyers. It was at this time that Billy Sharsig became involved in professional baseball. While Sharsig's father remained on Cadwalader Street, young William became a baseball manager and moved closer to his work (the playing grounds), first to 2031 North Ninth Street in 1883 and later to North Twenty-third Street. Sharsig's father moved to Fifth and Lehigh and, by 1891, was dead. Sharsig later moved to his Franklin Street home in the 1890s.

Before managing a pro team, Sharsig first managed well-known local clubs from Kensington, including the J.D. Shibe Club. As co-owner of the American Association's Athletics, Sharsig managed his team on several occasions: in 1886, and from 1888 to 1891. He finished his career with 238 wins and 216 losses for a .524 winning percentage. The Athletics won the American Association's pennant in 1883.

When today's American League was founded in 1901, Philadelphia's entry into the new league was a resurrection of the old Philadelphia Athletics. Fishtown's Benjamin F. Shibe and the legendary Connie Mack selected Billy Sharsig to look after the finances of the club.

Sharsig's new position as business manager of the Philadelphia Athletics would not last that long, as he died from stomach cancer at his home at 3044 Franklin Street on February 1, 1902. He was only forty-seven years old and had devoted most of his life to baseball. He was buried on February 5 at Mount Vernon Cemetery in Philadelphia. His funeral was attended by many of the most notable baseball figures of that era.

EDDY STANKY, PROFESSIONAL BASEBALL PLAYER, "THE BRAT FROM KENSINGTON"

Edward Raymond Stanky, nicknamed "The Brat from Kensington," was born on September 3, 1917, in Philadelphia. Eddie was born to German Russian parents in Kensington. His father was said to be a "frustrated semi-pro ballplayer" who worked as a leather glazer.

Between the years 1943 and 1953, Eddie Stanky played professional baseball for the Chicago Cubs (1943–44), Brooklyn Dodgers (1944–47), Boston Braves (1948–49), New York Giants (1950–51) and St. Louis Cardinals (1952–53). He played on pennant-winning teams with the Brooklyn Dodgers in 1947, the Boston Braves in 1948 and the New York Giants in 1951. It was Stanky who sparked the Giants' amazing pennant drive in 1951, with the Giants going 37-9 when Stanky returned to the lineup. Bobby Thompson's famous "Shot Heard Round the World" won the pennant for the Giants.

Edward Raymond Stanky (1917–1999), professional baseball player. Leo Durocher once stated, "He can't hit, can't run, can't field…all the little SOB can do is win."

In 1951, Stanky began coaching and managing baseball. He finished his playing career as a player-manager for the St. Louis Cardinals. He compiled a 467-435 record while coaching in the Majors for the St. Louis Cardinals (1952–55), Chicago White Sox (1966–68) and Texas Rangers (1977).

As a player, Stanky batted right handed and played second base. While not the greatest hitter (a career .268), he was able to execute all the little things that made him and the teams he played for winners. He was most famous for his ability to see the ball, as he led the National League three times in walks and had six seasons where he walked over 100 times each year (his 148 walks in 1945 was the NL record until broken by Barry Bonds in 1996). He was a three-time National League All-Star and led the league twice in on-base percentage. In 1945, he led the league in plate appearance with 726 and runs scored with 128. Stanky led the NL in sacrifice hits (20) in 1946, and in 1950, he led the NL in times on base (314). In 1946, he edged out Stan Musial for the league leader in on-base percentage, even though Musial led the league in 10-plus batting categories.

Stanky was an innovator in the game. He advocated for the designated hitter twenty years before the American League introduced it. He also had a tactic where if he was on third base and a fly ball was hit to the outfield, he would take several steps backward from third base into left field and then start to run and time when he would touch third base and the outfielder would catch the ball, thus giving Stanky full speed when running to home base. The league eventually outlawed this Stanky maneuver.

It's hard to stomach a Kensingtonian playing for New York, but Stanky's best season was his first year in New York, where he played 151 games, hit .300 for the season on 158 hits, scored 115 runs, walked 144 times and had an on-base percentage of .460. It was also in New York, in 1950, that he tied a Major League record by walking in seven straight plate appearances.

In all, Stanky played in 1,259 games, batted .268 on 1,154 hits, scored 811 runs and walked an amazing 996 times. His career on-base percentage was .410. He struck out only 374 times in eleven seasons.

After his professional baseball career was over, Stanky went on to a second career as the baseball coach for the University of South Alabama from 1969 to 1983. Stanky took over USA's unsuccessful baseball program in 1969 and compiled a 488-193 record in fourteen years. The University of South Alabama Jaguars won five NCAA tournaments, two Sun Belt Conference titles and two number-one rankings during Stanky's years at the helm.

In 1977, he retired briefly from coaching college baseball to coach the Texas Rangers; however, after one game (a win), he promptly quit because he was homesick for his family. He went back to USA and got his old job back coaching the Jaguars. On June 6, 1999, Stanky died of a heart attack in Fairhope, Alabama. He was eighty-three years old.

Stanky's father-in-law was Milt Stock (1893–1977), an infielder who also played professional baseball (1913–1926) for the New York Giants, Philadelphia Phillies, St. Louis Cardinals and Brooklyn Robbins.

Baseball legend Phil Rizzuto once said that Stanky "plays a snarling, dog-eat-dog kind of baseball." In his obituary, Stanky was called a "fiery second baseman" who helped three separate teams to win National League pennants. The famed Giants manager Leo Durocher once stated about his friend, "He can't hit, can't run, can't field…all the little SOB can do is win." Eddie Stanky, just another kid from Kensington.

Joseph T. Verdeur, Cedar Street's Gold Medalist Swimmer

Considered by many to be the greatest swimmer of the first half of the twentieth century, Joseph T. Verdeur (1926–1991) was a local neighborhood boy who lived for some time at 2551 Cedar Street, right between Sergeant and Hazzard Streets. His mother, Sophia, died in 1982, while living in the neighborhood.

Joe went to Northeast Catholic High School, where his swimming career first took off. Later, at LaSalle University, his swimming career excelled even further. He eventually came to be called the "King of the Medley," a difficult race requiring three different strokes. He acquired this moniker by being the AAU National Individual Medley champion for eight consecutive years (1943–50).

During his career, Verdeur held nineteen world records, twenty-one American records and twelve NCAA records. In 1948, he added an Olympic Gold Medal. In all, he won twenty AAU National Individual championships, four NCAA National Individual championships and was part of the AAU national championship team in 1944.

One of his best events was the butterfly, where he broke the world record twelve times between 1945 and 1950. Starting in 1943, he won

Joseph T. Verdeur (1926–1991), gold medalist, world record holder, greatest swimmer of the first half of the twentieth century. He lived at 2551 Cedar Street.

nine National AAU gold medals in the butterfly and ten AAU golds in the 200-meter breaststroke, to go with his already mentioned eight consecutive AAU National Individual Medley championships.

During his swimming days at LaSalle, before the era of the Pan-American Games or the Spring Championships, Verdeur took the NCAA Division I wins in the 200-yard butterfly in 1947 and 1948 with record times of 2:16.8 and 2:14.7, respectively. In 1949 and 1950, again for LaSalle, Verdeur took the win in the 150-meter individual medley clocking in at 1:30.8 and 1:31.2, respectively, both records for this relatively new event.

Verdeur's final triumph came when he took the gold medal in the 200-meter breaststroke at the 1948 Summer Olympics, held in London, England. The Olympics had been suspended during World War II, and these 1948 games were supposed to have been held in London back in 1944. If not for the cancellation, he would have competed and probably won in 1944 as well. Verdeur's gold medal in the 200-meter breaststroke came with an Olympic record-breaking time of 2:39.3.

One event in Verdeur's life can sum up the man. After he won the 200-meter breaststroke at the 1948 Olympics, he was set to race in the 4 x

200 freestyle, where he was certain to win another gold medal. Instead of racing, he allowed Wally Wolf to take his place, since Wolf had not raced yet. Wolf raced for the team event and won a gold medal. It's hard to imagine the athletes of today doing such an unselfish act.

Due to his amazing swimming career, Verdeur was easily elected in 1966 for the then recently opened International Swimming Hall of Fame and was one of its first honoree inductees.

Before graduating from LaSalle University in 1950, Verdeur swam for Northeast Catholic High School (Erie and Torresdale Avenues). The Falcons team won several titles during his years at Northeast. He graduated from Northeast in 1944 and was already a national breaststroke champion swimmer.

After his competitive swimming career, Verdeur married a Philadelphia woman, eventually fathering five children. He became a schoolteacher in the Philadelphia school district, teaching from 1954 to 1991. He is said to have taught gym for a while at the old Edison High School at Eighth and Lehigh. He also coached Temple University's swim team from 1960 to 1969, as well as Thomas Jefferson University's swim team from 1969 to 1981. To complement his swimming, teaching and coaching career, Verdeur also owned a pool supply company.

Verdeur moved to Bala Cynwyd, Pennsylvania, where he eventually died of cancer in 1991. He was sixty-five years old.

Besides being a swimming coach, Verdeur demanded excellence in academics as well. Supposedly he said, "Cs weren't good enough, whether it's in the classroom or in the swimming pool, you don't settle for anything less than your best." Besides being one of the greatest swimmers, "Verdeur's role as a teacher greatly influenced the lives of young people."

In the months leading up to the 1948 Olympics, Hollywood scouted Verdeur as a possible new "Tarzan." It is said that he wanted to play Tarzan and "had the looks to do it."

In May 1999, Verdeur was honored by LaSalle University with a bust of his likeness on the campus at Kirk Pool in Hayman Center.

Northeast Catholic, LaSalle, Temple, Thomas Jefferson and Tarzan—how much more Philadelphian can a fellow get? As then–LaSalle University president Nicholas Giordano said about Joe Verdeur, "The combination of superior athletic ability with selflessnes"—that was who Joe Verdeur was. Kensingtonians should be proud.

Bibliography

Most of the materials listed below are on the shelves at the Historical Society of Pennsylvania, the Philadelphia Free Library, Library Company of Philadelphia or are still in print. A couple of the items are in the possession of the author.

PUBLISHED SOURCES

Alcock, Sarah. *A Brief History of the Revolution with a Sketch of the Life of John Hewson*. Philadelphia: self-published, 1843.

Annual Reports of the Hospital of the Protestant Episcopal Church. Philadelphia: 1853–1863.

Catrambone, Jamie, and Harry C. Silcox., eds. *Kensington History: Stories and Memories*. Philadelphia: Brighton Press, 1996.

Custis, John Trevor. *The Public Schools of Philadelphia*. Philadelphia: Burk & McFetridge, Co., 1897.

A Directory of the Charitable, Social Improvement, Educational and Religious Associations and Churches of Philadelphia, prepared by the Civic Club. Philadelphia: 1903.

Dunham, A.C. "The Knights of Labor." *New Englander and Yale Review* 45, no. 195 (June 1886).

Gauer, David W. *Vaughan Shipwrights of Kensington, Philadelphia: Their Van Hook & Norris Lineages and Combined Progeny*. Decorah, IA: Anundsen Pub. Co., 1982.

Harrison, Joseph. *The Locomotive Engine, and Philadelphia's Share in its Early Improvements*. Philadelphia: George Gebbie, 1872.

Heckewelder, John, and Peter S. Duponceau. *An account of the history, manners and customs of the Indian nations who once inhabited Pennsylvania and the neighbouring states: A correspondence between the Rev. John Heckewelder...and Peter S. Duponceau...respecting the languages of the American Indians; Words, phrases and short dialogues in the language of the Lenni Lenape or Delaware Indians*. In *Transactions of the Historical & Literary Committee of the American Philosophical Society*, vol. 1. Philadelphia: A. Small, 1819.

Heinrich, Thomas R. *Ships for the Seven Seas: Philadelphia Shipbuilding in the Age of Industrial Capitalism*. Baltimore, MD: Johns Hopkins Press, 1997.

Lemay, Leo. *The Life of Benjamin Franklin*, vols. 1–3. Philadelphia: University of Pennsylvania Press, 2006–9.

Lindstrom, Peter. *Geographia Americae, with an introduction of the Delaware Indians based on Surveys and Notes made in 1654–1655*. Philadelphia: Swedish Colonial Society, 1925.

Milano, Kenneth W. *The History of the Kensington Soup Society*. Charleston, SC: The History Press, 2009.

———. *The History of Penn Treaty Park*. Charleston, SC: The History Press, 2009.

———. *Remembering Kensington & Fishtown*. Charleston, SC: The History Press, 2008.

Morton, Robert. "The Diary of Robert Morton. Kept in Philadelphia while that city was occupied by the British Army in 1777. *Pennsylvania Magazine of History & Biography* 1, no. 1 (1877).

Philadelphia Board of Health. Sanitary Committee Report, Philadelphia, 1849.

Philadelphia City Directories, various publishers, 1785–1936.

Philadelphia Stranger's Guide for 1825. Philadelphia: Thomas Wilson, 1825.

Prowell, George Reeser. *History of Camden County, New Jersey*. Philadelphia: Richards, 1886.

Remer, Rich. "Old Kensington." *Pennsylvania Legacies* 2, no. 2 (November 2002). Philadelphia: Historical Society of Pennsylvania, 2002.

Robson, Charles. *The Manufactories and Manufacturers of Pennsylvania in the Nineteenth Century*. Philadelphia: Galaxy Publishing Co., 1875.

Scharf, J. Thomas, and Thompson Westcott. *History of Philadelphia, 1609–1884*. 3 vols. Philadelphia: L.H. Everts & Co., 1884.

Schultz, Ronald. *The Republic of Labor; Philadelphia Artisans and the Politics of Class, 1720–1830*. New York: Oxford University Press, 1993.

Scranton, Philip. "Build a Firm, Start Another: The Bromleys and Family Firm Entrepreneurship in the Philadelphia Region." *Business History* 35, no. 4 (October 1993).

————. *Figured Tapestry: Productions, Markets, and Power in Philadelphia Textiles, 1885–1941*. Cambridge: Cambridge University Press, 1989.

————. *Proprietary Capitalism: The Textile Manufacture at Philadelphia, 1800–1885*. Cambridge: Cambridge University Press, 1983.

Simcoe, John Graves. *A. Simcoe's military journal: a history of the operations of a partisan corps, called the Queen's Rangers, commanded by Lieut. Col. J.G. Simcoe, during the war of the American Revolution.* New York: Bartlett & Welford, 1844.

Wallace, Paul A.W. *Indian Paths of Pennsylvania.* Harrisburg: Pennsylvania Historical and Museum Commission, 1998.

————. *Indians in Pennsylvania (Anthropological Series).* Harrisburg: Pennsylvania Historical and Museum Commission, 2nd Revised Edition, 2000.

Watson, John Fanning. *Annals of Philadelphia, and Pennsylvania, in the Olden Time; Being a Collection of Memoirs, Anecdotes, and Incidents of the City and its Inhabitants, and of the Earliest Settlements of the Inland Part of Pennsylvania.* Enlarged, with Many Revisions and Additions by Willis P. Hazard. 3 vols. Philadelphia: J.M. Stoddart & Co., 1879.

Webb, George. *Batchelor's-Hall; a Poem.* Philadelphia: printed and sold [by B. Franklin and H. Meredith] at the New Printing Office, 1731.

Weslager, C.A. *The Delaware Indians.* New Brunswick, NJ: Rutgers University Press, 1990.

UNPUBLISHED SOURCES

A.D. Marble & Company. "Phase IB/II Archaeological Investigation SugarHouse Casino Site" (36Ph137). Vols. 1 and 2. Philadelphia: February 2008, submitted to the U.S. Army Corps of Engineers. A copy is in possession of the author.

Bower, S.D.S. "Bower Family of Philadelphia." Located at Historical Society of Pennsylvania.

Dooley, James J. Journal of James A. Dooley, circa 1930. In possession of his granddaughter, Bonnie Dooley of Port Richmond, Philadelphia

Farmer, Elizabeth. Letterbook (1774–1777) (1783–1789). Located at Historical Society of Pennsylvania.

Hewson, John. Part of His Diary About His Escape from British to N.J. Sept. 20, 1778. Located at Historical Society of Pennsylvania.

Kensington History Project (Torben Jenk, Ken Milano and Rich Remer). "Response to Marble & Co.'s SugarHouse IBII Report" (February 2008). Philadelphia: Kensington History Project, 2008, submitted to the U.S. Army Crops of Engineers, Philadelphia. A copy is in the possession of the author.

Manuscript Minute Meetings of the A.C. Harmer Club. 1880–1900. In the possession of the author.

Records of the Philadelphia Public Bath Association, Philadelphia: 1895–1950. Located at the Historical Society of Pennsylvania.

INTERNET SOURCES

www.ancestry.com. A subscription website, containing the available United States Census, 1790–1930, as well as other sources.

www.genealogybank.com. An Internet subscription website, containing eighteenth-, nineteenth- and twentieth-century Philadelphia newspapers. This is a keyword searchable database. Much of the research on the Kensington Bank robbery, Cramp Shipyard strike, Philadelphia's labor lyceums, the Rusk twins and others of these articles were mined from this database.

www.kennethwmilano.com. Ken Milano's Encyclopaedia Kensingtoniana.

www.workshopoftheworld.com. Torben Jenk's Workshop of the World.

About the Author

Kenneth W. Milano was born and raised in Kensington and still lives in that section of Philadelphia, where his mother's German ancestors first arrived from Unterleichtersbach, Bavaria, in the early 1840s.

He is a graduate of St. Anne's Grammar School, Northeast Catholic High School and Temple University. Before attending Temple University, Ken served a four-year apprenticeship as a marine painter at the old Philadelphia Naval Shipyard.

After college, Milano taught GED and ESL classes for eight years at Lutheran Settlement House in Kensington, where he met and married Dorina Lala, formerly of Fier, Albania. They have two boys, Francesco and Salvatore.

Ken also has a twenty-plus-year history in the rare and scholarly bookselling and manuscript business. He currently works with the bookselling firm of Michael Brown Rare Americana, LLC, of Philadelphia, and received his training under Mr. George R. Allen, of the legendary Philadelphia firm of William H. Allen, Booksellers.

In the mid-1990s, Mr. Milano, along with Rich Remer and Torben Jenk, helped to found the Kensington History Project, a community-based historical group that researches, lectures and publishes on the history of Kensington and Fishtown.

Visit us at
www.historypress.net